Comments of Students From
Write From the Heart Workshops

"Thanks for allowing me to get a tiny but powerful glimpse of the wellspring of creativity that I have inside!"— D.H.

"Taking your workshop has changed my life and continues to do so every day, as I pick up my pen or sit down at the computer to see what comes out."— A.B.

"This has been a gift to my mind, my heart and my spirit. . . . As I wrote my own stories I learned to consciously enter that realm where the words flow from a deep inner source . . ."— M.K.

"I felt that I . . . emerged with something genuinely wonderful. It was such a glorious feeling that I want to repeat it over and over again . . . has encouraged me about my writing and reawakened in me my dream of truly communicating my experiences and insights through the written word."— J.F.

"I learned a great deal about myself, my relation to the world, and who I am as a writer. I developed an intimacy to my writing, learned to get close to the bone, to expose my soul, to tell the truth with clarity and genuineness."— L.S.

Praise for the Books of Hal Bennett

"Provocative . . . discovering the bliss that results from self-realization. Great reading!"
Wayne Dyer, author of Real Magic

"It's fun to believe this book is a first light of dawn . . ."
Richard Bach, author of Jonathan Livingston Seagull

"Hal Bennett is a gifted writer. He generously shares the secrets of good writing in Write from the Heart."
Shakti Gawain, author of The Path of Transformation

"Hal is becoming one of my favorite authors."
Lynn Andrews, author of Medicine Woman

"Hal Bennett's ground-breaking work in the journalism of consciousness over the past two decades has influenced many."
Michael Toms, New Dimensions Radio

"A wonderfully lucid and intelligent book, full of fascinating insights."
Gabrielle Roth, author of Maps to Ecstasy

"Write From the Heart offers a new way to look at writing . . . reminding us that through the miracle of language we can embrace and share the wisdom of our hearts."
Gerald Jampolsky, author of Love is Letting Go of Fear

Christmas '99

Dearest Mom,

I'm so proud of who you are and all you do. Thank you for setting a wonderful example as a determined, strong woman. May all of your dreams come true — except that "grandmother at 47" thing. I love you,
Greta

This book is about writing
. . . from your heart.

And it's about finding
the Creative Spirit
that lives within each of us.

*It's for anyone
who loves writing—
whether
a private journal . . .*

Or a book
of nonfiction . . .

*Or the first pages
of the world's greatest
yet-to-be-published novel . . .*

Or a single poem . . .

Or maybe just in your mind.

Write from the Heart

Unleashing the Power
of Your Creativity

HAL ZINA BENNETT

with a special section
on getting happily published

Nataraj Publishing
a division of
New World Library
Novato, CA

Nataraj Publishing
a division of

New World Library
14 Pamaron Way
Novato, CA 94949

Edited by Hal Zina Bennett
Cover art and design by Greg Wittrock
Cover photo by Emma Hooker Photography, Inc.
Typography by TBH/Typecast, Inc.

Library of Congress Cataloging-in-Publication Data

Bennett, Hal Zina, 1936-
   Write from the heart: unleashing the power of your creativity/
by Hal Zina Bennett
      p. cm.
   Includes bibliographical references.
   ISBN 1-88259-27-5 (alk.paper)
   1. Authorship. 2. Creativity—Psychological aspects. 1. Title.
PN151.B514   1995
808'.02—dc20   95-18857
                           CIP

ISBN 1-882591-27-5

Printed in U.S.A.

10 9 8 7 6 5 4 3

Dedicated to Susan J. Sparrow, for her patience and humor, but mostly for her quiet wisdom, constant love, and partnership.

Acknowledgments

For most readers, a book is the work of its author. But for the author, no book is possible without the help and dedication of a long list of people.

First, I'd like to thank Shakti Gawain and Jane "Melody" Hogan, without whose shared vision Nataraj Publishing could never have come to be. What they have co-created is a rare treasure in today's publishing world.

Next, thanks to everyone on the Nataraj team staff who had a hand in ushering this book from idea to final product—Jim Burns, Elizabeth Youngquist, Lora O'Connor, Uma Ergil, Theresa Nelson, Susan Ward, and Sue Mann.

From out in the wings—prompting, fomenting, and often grabbing one or the other of us by the hand (usually the left one) and leading us through the darkness—I would like to thank Kathy Altman and Lori Salzman, the two right hands of Right Hand Productions.

I'd like to thank Greg Wittrock for a wonderful cover, and Bill Turner at TBH/Typecast for the roles he played in producing a book that is attractive and accessible.

Thanks to Reid Tracy, Jeannie Liberati, and the staff at Hay House, without whose efforts this book would never get into the hands of the readers.

My sincere thanks to all my students and writing clients over the years, far too numerous to list here, whose contributions show up in so many ways on the pages of this book.

Finally, my special thanks to Bob Frager, who suggested I teach this work at the Institute of Transpersonal Psychology. My deep appreciation, also, for his creation of a truly magical setting where thousands of students, as well as teachers, have been able to explore and touch a Greater Reality.

Contents

In Search of the Creative Source

Our creativity is not a cute thing for weekend dabblers in the arts; it lies at the essence of who we are. We are all creators, and therefore we all have work—good work—awaiting us.

MATTHEW FOX

Friends who knew me in my childhood say I was a very strange little boy. I spent those early years in the suburbs of Detroit, back when most midwestern suburbs were still surrounded by working farms, open fields, and relatively untouched stretches of woodlands. My parents built their dream home on a quiet road, way beyond sidewalks and paved streets. The road that went by our house was oiled gravel, which meant that once or twice a year a grungy truck from the county lumbered through our neighborhood, spraying watery black creosote on the gravel to keep down the summer dust. Although my father drove thirty miles to a city job every day, we had more than a half-acre of land, where we kept a few laying hens and planted a vegetable garden every spring.

Judging by my memory and the stories I've been told, I lived in a world all my own. I was a dreamer. My parents were afraid that someday I'd get hit by a car for lack of proper attention to the *real* world. I remember it differently. I recall things like climbing trees in the forested area behind our home and just sitting there, ensconced on a limb thirty feet above the ground and rocked by a gentle breeze. I noticed early on that when I immersed myself in that world, surrounded by nature, and didn't move a muscle, birds and other wildlife no longer noticed me and would go about their business as if I wasn't there. When that happened, my attention shifted and I became very still inside, particularly in the spring and early fall when I could nestle in, hugging the barky trunk and looking out through a curtain of brightly colored leaves.

It isn't that I was all that interested in nature. More than anything else I enjoyed the profound solitude of those moments, away from the house where it seemed there was always a level of busy-ness that took me too far out of myself. Years later, when I first read Robert Frost's poem, "Birches," I immediately knew what he meant when he talked about the boy who grew up, "too far from town to learn baseball,/ Whose only play was what he found himself." Even though I wasn't far from town, I never did learn baseball, no doubt because other things interested me more. I regretted that at times, mostly when I was excluded from neighborhood games and sulked back home with my head down. But I continued to find greater satisfaction and excitement in the creative process, long before I knew enough to call it that.

When I relive those early years, I begin to appreciate what good training they were for a writer. First, I think, they impressed upon me a deep appreciation for the opulent luxuries of solitude, too often neglected in the frenzy of modern life. And second, those years gave me time to unhurriedly explore the magic of the inner world, from which we draw the themes and rich imagery that give our creative efforts their originality.

If those years served me well, they also taught me something that has been invaluable in my work with other writers. It is that most of the skills required by this craft are commonplace. And the magic ingredient so many of us writers seek—that which will allow us to turn our dreams of becoming successful writers into the real thing—is always right under our noses. For example, much of that ingredient starts with solitude, with the experience of sitting quietly until we are welcomed into our own inner worlds.

As simple as that sounds, it's also something that we trade for the lesser pleasures of modern life, like Walkman radios people wear on their heads even on hiking trails in the wilderness. I often wonder if learning solitude wouldn't, in the long run, be a better skill to teach schoolchildren than grammar exercises and algebra, which most of us forget all too quickly anyhow. Although my parents always assured me that I was offered excellent educational opportunities—with the implication that I hadn't taken advantage of them—I cannot recall a teacher who even suggested that there was value in solitude. On the contrary, people who spent too much time looking inward were generally thought to be just a step or two from the funny farm.

When I sat down to write this book, I knew that the central message I had to convey to other writers was that the most valuable asset we have in this vocation is ourselves. Even the best writers seem to require constant reminders of that. There are a million books out there that teach writing techniques, things like how to create characters, how to develop a focused theme, how to write dialogue, or how to organize your book. All of this has its place, of course, but I also know that I share the frustration with other people who finish reading those books or come away from writing workshops that focus on techniques with a kind of longing—of wanting something more.

The *something more* I always wanted when I started writing had to do with questions like these: Where do I look for the imagery and themes that I can feel truly passionate about? Where do I find ideas so thoroughly engaging that the sheer momentum of my fascination will propel me forward to fill the two or three hundred pages it takes to make a book? How can I truly make a contribution through my writing? What is my gift and my mission?

When we love books, it's doubly difficult to answer these questions. We wander through the aisles of a library or our favorite bookstores and think, Is there really anything new under the sun? Is there really something I have to add to all this? I must confess that while walking through the stacks, or even searching through my helter-skelter bookshelves, I do ask those questions. Certainly there are many minds with far more to say than I. But when I start feeling sorry for myself, vowing that I will never write another word, I hear the voice of the spiritual teacher who told me, "There is nothing new under the sun—except you!"

His point was that each of us who dares to reach in and pull out what is truly ourselves brings a new way of seeing into the world. You may not be saying something that multitudes before you haven't said, but the *way* you say it, the particular spin you put on it, colored and tempered by your unique life experience, allows some to hear it for the first time. And that's the only justification I have found for climbing out on that precarious, swaying limb that writing requires of us.

To thine own self be true is probably the oldest and most ubiquitous saying in all religious and philosophical teaching. And there's no doubt in my mind that the profession of writing calls upon us over and over to be true to ourselves. Being true to ourselves is what gives our writing fire. It's what lights our lights when we're reading. But it's also the one thing we humans are only beginning to learn.

I believe that we don't have to be experts at the art of self-knowledge to be good writers—or even good people, for that matter. Knowing ourselves about ten percent of the time seems about as close as most of us get. And that seems to be enough. That ten percent, like the infinitesimal specks of pollen that cling to a bee's wings, can beautify and nourish the world if we dare risk it.

Over the past three decades that I've been writing professionally, I've seen a new style of writing emerging—in fiction, nonfiction, poetry, and journals—that uses lessons about self-truths in a new way. It seems that we're finally recognizing that nobody can ever be the final authority on anything. To share our humanness—that is, what we've encountered on our life paths—turns out to be far more valuable than claiming we have discovered ultimate truths or even that we've come up with something truly original.

If this book does nothing else, I hope it will say something to every reader about the process for opening to our own uniqueness. I hope it shines some light on that too often hidden part within each one of us that holds the rich imagery and themes and life experiences and wizardry that makes writing such a powerful medium. Study your writing techniques, but never forget, even for a moment, to be true to yourself, to honor the wondrous treasures you yourself embody.

Greater and greater numbers of people are seeking ways to throw open the gates to their creativity. Many have found that writing can do that. Even in the past ten years, men and women from all walks of life have become enchanted by the power of words and the inner worlds we can discover through them. Some write novels, some write poetry, some write non-fiction; others are content to confine their work to their private journals. I have found it fascinating to watch this great groundswell of interest in writing and creativity, and I think it is no accident that it has paralleled the growth of the recovery movement and what has been called a spiritual renaissance in our country. We are all seeking greater meaning in our lives, and for many people creativity represents a kind of golden grail promising a sense of personal fulfillment and healing that nothing else can.

I like what Matthew Fox said, not so much about writing per se but about the creative act in general: "Creativity is the link between our inner work and the outer work that society requires of us. Creativity is the threshold through which our non-action leads to actions of beautification, celebration, and healing in the world. Creativity is both an inner work *and* an outer work."

One thing is certain: Few of us think of creativity as a frivolous activity or as something only self-indulgent "arty" people take seriously. We recognize that it nurtures us, at a time when humanity is very much in need of a spiritual boost. There's a new appreciation for our creative efforts as a way to bring us all a little closer to ourselves and in doing so renew the spirit of humankind.

In my work with other writers, I think what has most interested me is having them reveal to me their private thoughts about what they believed to be the vital source of their creativity.

It is clear to me that those who have been most successful in writing are people who recognized the gifts of their life experiences and discovered how to shape that material into artifacts that could make lasting impacts on their readers. There is, after all, nothing that we can ever hope to know better than our own life experiences. Buckminster Fuller once said, "I am the only guinea pig I have," suggesting something the creative person understands only too well, that everything that happens to us is potentially raw material for anything we might write. Fuller was addressing a convention of engineers at the time, but I see the concept as one that perhaps even more accurately applies to writers.

There are great mysteries spun around what many have described as our creative wellsprings, the source from which our passions, our inspiration, and our imagery comes. But too often the subject of creativity and inspiration leaves us more bewildered than informed, leaving us with the impression that the creative spirit is a distant angel who has to be teased into our lives, manipulated and seduced into serving us. Through my experiences, I am convinced that our most powerful creative sources are far more accessible and are incidentally, far more down to earth.

We each have within us many characters: children, adults, playmates, animals, wise counselors. The cast of characters is endless. We have only to consider our dreams, peopled with characters of all shapes, sizes, colors, and convictions, for evidence that this is true. It is through the exploration of our inner world that we find the roots of our unique voice and our creativity. And yet, in a way that is virtually impossible to explain, after attaining our own voice and learning to draw from our own creative source, we see and hear not only how we are each unique but how we are all the same. We glimpse the single, unifying consciousness that makes us one. That is, what is most idiosyncratically you allows you to look beyond what is most idiosyncratically me, and together we can view the brilliant hues of that blazing universal horizon where our experience of life is exactly the same.

I am convinced there is such a thing as divine inspiration. In the final analysis it is undoubtedly the most powerful source of our creativity. However, even this is accessible to all of us. I have watched writers of every age and every level of expertise tap into this source—surprising even themselves—through concentrating on the very personal and individual sources I've just discussed.

If all this seems a bit obscure, don't worry. The stories I'll be sharing with you will, I hope, make these ideas more clear and accessible.

There are many processes—I hate calling them *techniques*—I have learned to use in my own writing that I have passed along to my writing students. Whenever possible, I'll share their stories with you, which I think are at least as valuable as my own. When you take all these anecdotes as a whole, this book, in effect, turns out to be a kind of chorus of voices, collectively much bigger than my own.

I trust that the songs we sing will inspire you to join in!

I: Born to Write

When we choose a goal and invest ourselves in it to the limits of our concentration, whatever we do will be enjoyable. And once we have tasted this joy, we will redouble our efforts to taste it again. This is the way the self grows.

MIHALY CSIKSZENTMIHALYI

Every once in a while someone asks me if I think there's such a thing as a born writer. Although I suppose there is, my bet is that born writers are few and far between. I wouldn't count myself as one. Most writers I know regard their abilities as being hard won, certainly not something they came into life knowing. However, my friend Ken says there was a moment in his childhood when he knew he was destined to be an author. At ten years of age he won a library competition for a short story he wrote. They gave him a fifty-dollar U.S. Savings Bond and a little bronze plaque with his name and the title of his story etched on it.

Ken's story was published in his hometown newspaper, along with a photograph of him clutching the plaque to his chest with his right hand and holding up the savings bond with his left. His English teacher took him aside after he got his award and encouraged him to pursue a career in journalism, telling him how terrible it would be if he wasted his God-given talent. Ken told me that even then he considered a journalism career to be selling himself short because he'd always dreamed of writing books that would be printed in hardcover and shelved in the public library. But he didn't tell his teacher that.

Ken's story was about a kid who wanted to play baseball more than anything in his life. There was a Little League team in his town, and one day at school his friend asked if he'd like to join. But the kid in the story said no. The truth was that he knew his parents couldn't afford the equipment he'd have to buy. They were farm workers and very poor. But he continued to practice, throwing an old softball at a target he'd painted on the door of an abandoned truck down in a gravel pit on the farm where he and his parents lived. One day the boy's uncle saw him pitching the ball like that and thought he was pretty good. That night he took his nephew aside and gave him a crisp twenty-dollar bill to buy the equipment he needed to join the league.

After he won the prize from the library, and had his picture and his story published in the paper, Ken wondered if maybe he should have told them that the story was mostly true. It was about himself. The only part he'd made up was the part about the uncle who gave him the twenty-dollar bill. For years he felt guilty about accepting the prize, until he learned that most of the world's great writers also drew their stories from life.

Last year Ken and I met for coffee at a little place on Potrero Hill in San Francisco. We get together about once a year to catch up on each other's lives and talk about writing.

I've always looked up to Ken because of his literary accomplishments. When we first met we were enrolled in the creative writing program at San Francisco State University, and he already had a novel about half-done. He was legendary in the department. Before we graduated he'd won two or three prestigious writing grants and an editor at Knopf was negotiating for his first book.

About a year after we graduated, Ken called to say that he'd signed a contract and his novel was coming out in about a year. We agreed to meet for dinner the following week, but he canceled at the last minute. His agent (he now had a literary agent!) had been talking with a Hollywood producer who wanted to make a film of his book. They were flying Ken to Spain, where the producer had a summer home, so that they could discuss what Ken's role would be. Ken was insisting on being the script writer, insurance against the filmmaker straying too far from the original story.

Ken and I didn't get together for nearly two years. I was alternately jealous and happy for him, awed by his achievement and wondering why I hadn't yet been similarly blessed. In my mind he'd become bigger than life, and I soon developed a strange fear of him that I always have about celebrities. Around friends I bragged that I knew him, but the distance between Ken and me grew until we were nearly strangers.

His book came out and critics heralded him as "the next John Steinbeck." He signed on with the movies, wrote the script and sat through the entire production, a watchdog protecting his integrity. When the film was released a year later, the critics were generous, calling it "a new American classic."

For a while Ken lived well, yet modestly, off his royalty income. But that was more than twenty-five years ago. He has written only one film script since then, based on a short story he had written when we were still students. I remembered the story well because I had published it in the literary quarterly I was editing at the time. I liked the story and I liked the film. But the movie went nowhere, even though it was a good movie, because the distributors didn't like it. Distributors, Ken explained, will only take films with big-name actors. His film had excellent acting but no big-name actors.

The last time we had coffee, Ken confessed that he hadn't written anything he considered significant since his first novel. He said that he didn't even feel inspired anymore. He asked me how I managed to keep writing. Though I published mostly nonfiction, he said that he liked what I wrote because my books always seemed inspired. He wanted to know where I found that inspiration. How did I keep coming up with it year after year and book after book? I couldn't say just then, but when I got home that night I started thinking about our conversation that day.

Ken was one of those people who could tell you the exact moment when they knew they would become writers. And there's no denying that he had done it. He had one excellent novel and two good film scripts to prove it. But, I had to wonder, was that the whole thing? It's as if he loaded his creative cannon at age ten, the day he learned that he'd won the short story contest, fired it off at age twenty-nine, made some big sparks—and that was it. Whatever creative charge drove him to write his novel was used up in more or less a single shot.

Maybe it's the nature of legends to go out in one big flash. Certainly the literary world is replete with such stories. But I have to say that as sadly romantic as they may be, these stories have ceased to interest me except perhaps as warnings.

I can't say I don't feel sorry for Ken and others like him, but I think that I mostly feel impatient, maybe even irritated. If I have literary heroes these days, which I do, they are of a different ilk. Most come from workshops I've taught or from stories people share with me when we talk about writing.

I don't know whether there is a new kind of writer in the world today or if I have just discovered something that has been there all along. I think about Sharon, a retired nun, who signed up for her first writing class at the age of sixty-seven. Timid and unsure of herself, she read what she claimed was the first short story she'd written, dutifully fulfilling the task I'd assigned. In the story she told about a recent visit to her hometown in Canada, which she had left when she was a teenager. She went to look for the house where she'd been born. Instead she found a vacant lot where the family home once stood. There were only waist-high weeds now and a shallow foundation filled with rubble. She described a single sunflower, about six feet tall with a flower as big as a Cadillac hubcap, standing like a guardian over what had once been the front steps.

Reflecting on that empty lot, Sharon took us deep inside her soul, revealing a history of pain, hardship, and joy, of early loves and prohibitions, of victories and disappointments, and of old wounds that even after sixty years had only begun to heal. In twenty minutes she took us on a journey deep into a life that somehow stood for all our lives, showing how human experience lives on in our hearts long after all physical evidence of it has been erased from the earth.

As she finished reading, the room fell silent. When she looked up it was with an anxious smile, like a child who didn't know what she'd done and was waiting for a sign that would tell her. Across from her a man in his thirties sat hugging his knees, trying not to cry.

Sharon finally screwed up her courage enough to say, "Well?"

"You'll have to give us all a minute to recover," I said.

"Was it that bad?" she asked.

"No," somebody said. "It was that good!"

The last time I spoke with Sharon, she was working on a collection of short stories. And if I were a publisher I can assure you I'd have handed her a contract that day. We talked about writing and I told her again how deeply I'd been touched by that first story she'd read at the workshop.

"I learned a lot that day," she said.

"What, that you are a writer?"

She blushed. "Well, I don't know what it really means to be a writer," she said. "But I did discover how wonderful it is to write. It dissolves barriers I thought could never be dissolved."

What she said reiterated a truth I've seen expressed many times in writing workshops that too often goes unnoticed. It happens at those moments when we forget our literary pretensions and let language do what I have an idea the inventor of the universe intended it to do: help us bridge between one consciousness and another and help us connect with the larger consciousness that embraces everything.

There's something sad and even dangerous about a society that loses touch with this basic understanding, that either puts writing on a pedestal or uses it to exploit and manipulate.

We talked about publishing, and Sharon said, "I don't know as I could ever think of myself as a writer, but one day I'd like to have my work published so that I could go around the country and read my stories to people."

I know what she means. I sometimes think that in a past life I must have been the storyteller of a small tribe. When the pressures of publishers' deadlines and arguments with editors start crowding me, I sometimes dream how great it would be just to tell stories to a small circle of friends and neighbors who've gathered around a campfire. And there's no doubt in my mind that we have a lot to learn from those early storytellers, who measured their success by whether or not their stories unveiled previously hidden truths that would improve all their lives, even as they entertained. We'll discuss this concept more in chapter eleven.

Sometimes I think my friend Ken lost sight of what writing is all about. He got seduced by the ivory tower and forgot that being a writer is really something much more than being the literary critics' darling. I don't know what he thought might happen to his life after he published his novel. Whatever it was he dreamed obviously never came true for him. And what did happen—fame, fortune, kudos from the most respected critics—didn't work for him.

When language is working for us, the way I think it does for Sharon, it touches something ancient and even primordial and pure in us—if we're open at all to it happening. It's a path into a territory so essential and so elemental that when we're in there we feel as if we've come home. It's a place where individual behaviors and different tongues, races, and genders, to say nothing of religious and nationalistic identities, cease to divide us. And it's a place where even our harshest self-judgments disappear.

Generally, when it happens, it is a fleeting glimpse, as startling as the glowing eyes of a nocturnal creature that dashes off to the side of the road to escape the bright beams of our car's headlights as we race through the night. But as fleeting as these moments may be, they can also change our lives forever. They can happen whether we are writing the great American novel or an entry in our private journals. It is moments like these that we yearn to experience in writing, and I'm sure this yearning is the fuel that drives us to put pen to paper.

Rilke said, "We are only mouth. Who sings the distant heart that dwells entire within all things?" The poet was reflecting on the Logos, the Word, as in St. John's Gospel: "When all things began, the Word already was. The Word dwelt with God, and what God was, the Word was."

Although I am not a religious scholar, those lines have always intrigued me, just as they apparently did Rilke. Some years ago I stumbled upon a book by Georg Kuhlewind, an obscure but stimulating writer who was a proponent of Rudolph Steiner's anthroposophy, a twentieth-century religious system growing out of theosophy and centering on human development. While exploring St. John's writings, Kuhlewind came to believe that the Word "is truly the primal beginning. As soon as something moves, to do something or to *think*, the Word is there and, with it, the beginning." His point is that because all that moves or thinks comes from the Logos (the Word), we are ultimately all joined as one through it. He says, "Without the Logos, there would not be even the attempt to communicate, nor any claim to communication."

Who can say if this is true or not? I tend to believe that philosophers spend too much time and energy trying to figure things out. Soon they begin to believe themselves and can no longer tell the difference between their stories and the larger truth they're trying to comprehend. What matters to me in Kuhlewind's speculations is the possibility that language is much more than we think it is. If it's true that all begins with the Word, then maybe what so deeply moves us about writing is that it somehow connects us with our primal source. That spark of recognition and connectedness that we experience when we're really on isn't an illusion. And the drive we feel to write something really stunning and glorious isn't self-indulgent or something akin to addictive behavior. Rather, what excites us is the recognition that our writing literally builds bridges between our consciousness—our life experience—and that of at least one other person. And beyond that we've tapped into that little piece of the Logos we each hold within us, the creative source from which we all come.

There are probably religious leaders who will tell me I'm crazy or that I'm wrenching the text and treading on dangerous ground. But I don't agree. I believe there is a part of writing that's divine, that connects us with a greater authority than ourselves. And that, certainly, is something we're all born with. If that makes us born writers, so be it. The promise is that we can learn to tap into that potential at virtually any point in our lives, trusting that the Word lives in us. Who dares to claim the prize will have it.

2: Why We Must Write

His (the writer's) function is to make his imagination theirs (the readers') and he fulfills himself only as he sees his imagination become the light in the minds of others. His role, in short, is to help people live their lives.

WALLACE STEVENS

Words have always been magical and nourishing for me, perhaps because some of my fondest childhood memories involve books. Until my brother and I were about eight years old, mother always read to us at bedtime. In those moments before I slipped off to sleep, vast worlds unfolded in my mind peopled with marvelous characters, some human, some animals, all from other times and other places. In those imaginative journeys, I experienced a sense of adventure and wonder. Immersed in those worlds I found love and fear, compassion and conflict. The words formed images that became enchanted paths into the minds and hearts of people I had never met. And in those moments I began to believe that it might be possible to also share the inner experiences of real people in real life, beyond the pages of books. Life opened to me through the thoughts, feelings, characters, and places that the stories somehow shaped in my brain. Out of the spectacular make-believe of books I began to create a vision of what my life could become.

I was intrigued and thrilled by the worlds those early books opened up to me. At eight or nine years of age, I read my first "big" book, a beautiful hardcover of *Treasure Island*, complete with hand-tinted color plates, that my parents had given me for Christmas. By then my mother and father had started a family business and my mother had stopped reading to us in the evenings. She had a small antique and gift shop downtown and would come home at night too tired to carry on the bedtime routine my brother and I had always so deeply enjoyed. But she started bringing home the Hardy Boys mysteries, which launched me into a reading frenzy that took me through the entire series over the next two or three years.

Television became popular when I was about ten, but until that time we had radio, which still depended on the power of language to carry the story. I clearly recall my best friend, Mike, and I lying on the living room floor in front of a giant Philco radio with a huge speaker behind a mahogany grill. Out of that speaker came words and sounds that carried us into other worlds. Every afternoon, right after school, we listened to the adventure programs for kids: "Captain Midnight," " Batman," " The Lone Ranger," and "Tom Mix." Words painted pictures in my mind and caused people to come alive in the limitless landscape of my young imagination.

Today, when I start to write I remember those early years, and they remind me of what a miracle language really is. There are times, of course, when in the middle of writing I set my work aside in utter frustration, unable to get the words to do what I am experiencing in my mind. But even at those moments there is still wonder and awe for me in writing, a special pleasure I am certain I will never lose.

Having written for a living most of my adult life, I've done a lot of thinking about language. And I have asked myself many times what it is that so intrigues me about it. There are those who get the same charge out of music or art. There are those, like my wife, who find the same delight growing beautiful and exotic flowers. And there are those whose bliss is science, seeking the elusive secrets of the universe.

I know that it is not words per se or the structure of language that intrigues me so much. I have always been rather indifferent to the rules that govern the way we put words on paper. More than anything else, it is the marriage between language and the deep mysteries of the mind that excites me. How is it that with words we can move others to tears or laughter, or even communicate a complex scientific principle? Behind the words we find the human consciousness itself—that marvelous instrument without which language would have no meaning.

As lonely and frustrating as the writer's journey can be at times, I can't think of any vocation I'd trade for it. Over the years I've known and worked with hundreds of writers, men and women of all ages who eat, breathe, and dream writing like people addicted to an exotic drug. They all have stories to tell about the thrill of producing their first poem, short story, novel, or essay. And I have seen lives transformed as the dream of becoming an author was transformed into a reality through the publication of a book.

Not all get famous. Not all get rich—in fact, few in this business ever do. But there's no denying that our lives take on another dimension when we get into print. I suppose that's one of the most seductive parts of being an author because at the point when we're published we often discover—sometimes shockingly—the other side of the writing experience. We discover that as intrigued as we may have been by the process of writing itself, an entire, new experience is now unfolding as we discover that we are actually being read—not just by our mothers or our best friends, who adore us and would never say what they really think of our writing, but by thousands of strangers.

I remember my first published book. It was a mystery story, no doubt inspired by my early reading of the Hardy Boys series, for a publisher who specialized in high-interest books for sixth graders through junior high schoolers. Writing the story and then working with the editor was a much longer and arduous task than I could have imagined. By the time it was done I was so tired of seeing my words that I almost didn't care if I ever saw them again. But the day my editor called to say he had just received a box of books from the printer and I could pick up my complimentary copies, my heart battered in my ribcage. I raced across town in my car, probably running a couple of stoplights in the process and nearly taking the life of a pedestrian.

At my publisher's a copy of my first book was pressed into my trembling hands. It was a thin hardcover with a picture of a fishing boat on the cover, depicting the locale where the story took place. I had never known or even thought about the cover art, but it was a pleasant surprise, to say the least. I opened the book and pressed it to my face, deeply inhaling the scent of fresh ink on new paper. Then, turning to the first page I read my words in print for the first time, and in that moment

I felt something shift in the way I saw the world and particularly in how I thought about myself. Becoming an author was no longer a fantasy. I had done it! I had really and truly stepped into the life that until then had existed only in my wildest dreams.

I think it took me nearly a year to get used to thinking of myself as an author. To tell you the truth, I still have trouble with that concept from time to time, even after publishing numerous books. But there was no denying the wonderful, if daunting, truth. I could hold the book in my hand, or occasionally read a page or two from it, and feel a certain thrill and sense of accomplishment that I'd never before enjoyed. But it was not until I was asked to read from it as part of a library program for young people that I grasped the full significance of being a published author.

I was terribly nervous the day of the reading. All sorts of fantasies ran through my head. Most of them were disturbing, such as the voice that said to me, "You're not a *real* author! Who do you think you are getting up and pretending such a thing in front of a bunch of kids?" I think this came from old conditioning, when I was told by my parents and teachers that I was not much of a student and should probably seek employment as a factory worker or salesman. But on the appointed morning, still steeped in self-doubt, I faced a roomful of children in that musty room in the downtown San Francisco Public Library and heard the librarian introducing me, telling about the exciting story I had written and that I would be reading it to them.

With voice quavering and knees shaking behind the podium, I began reading, careful not to look up from the page for fear of seeing their faces and losing my nerve. Five minutes into the story, however, I noticed that the room had become deathly quiet. I put my finger on the page so that I wouldn't lose my place, then looked up. What I saw amazed me. All eyes were on me, faces intent, some with jaws dropped open in awe. I realized then that they were completely caught up in my story.

It took me about forty-five minutes to read the book, editing out two or three parts when the action bogged down a little. When I had finished, hands shot up from the crowd of young listeners; they wanted to know what happened to this character or that *afterward*. Was the main character's mother scared when the teenaged hero was kidnapped for two days? When he grew up, did the hero get a boat and become a fisherman like his father?

I realized my budding young readers had been completely convinced that the world I had created was real. To them the people I'd shaped from my fantasies were as real as their best friends or family members. They cared about them and wanted to know more about their lives. I tried to explain that the story was fiction, but somehow they didn't seem convinced. Through my words I had created a world of people and situations that mattered to them as much as their daily lives did.

I came away from that reading with a very different perspective about my writing. Beyond the thrill of publishing my first book was the realization that what we create with our words can have a real impact on other people's lives. It is as if through our words we enter their minds. We mingle our own inner worlds with our readers', in many cases touching their lives in ways that will change them forever.

In spite of my early success writing children's stories, it quickly became clear to me that if I was to survive economically in the world of publishing I'd better turn to nonfiction. In any case, I never had any great illusions about writing the great American novel or a philosophical treatise that would revolutionize human thought. Within the next five years, writing only at night after work, I completed and had three more books published, two of them fiction and one nonfiction. Then, following a motorcycle accident that hospitalized me for two months, I became obsessed with the idea of writing a popular medical book. While in the hospital I'd noticed that people who were injured or ill seemed to surrender all their power, and their responsibility for their health, to their physicians. Part of the problem, it seemed to me, was that people didn't know enough about their bodies or about medicine to ask intelligent questions.

After recovering from the accident, I began looking for a doctor with whom to write a book that would empower people to take charge of their health. This was in the late 1960s, long before the standard health section now found in most bookstores. At the time most stores carried two health books: *The Red Cross First Aid Manual* and a huge, forbidding hardcover called *The Better Homes and Garden Home Medical Encyclopedia*. Most publishers thought my idea crazy, as did most doctors I talked to while looking for potential collaborators.

Then, in 1970 I met Mike Samuels, a doctor who also believed there was a need for a "friendly" book that would give people the information they needed to take greater responsibility for their health. The book would challenge some sacred cows and traditions that had been upheld in our culture for nearly a century, but our main goal was to demystify personal health and build a new model for wellness. We found a publisher and wrote it in nine months—originally, a seven-hundred-page manuscript—nearly destroying our health in the process. Within eighteen months from the beginning of the project we had finished books rolling into the stores. It was an oversized yellow book with a colorful hand-rendered caduceus on the cover. We called it *The Well Body Book.* Unbeknownst to us at the time it would prove, in the next couple of years, to be a pivotal book, initiating a new genre of books and supporting a revolutionary way of thinking about our bodies.

When that book first came out, we toured colleges and bookstores throughout the West, talking about our concepts, even demonstrating how people could take their blood pressure, test their urine, and do their pelvic exams. We taught relaxation techniques, discussed the role of physical exercise and health, and even how to diagnose and treat common diseases. At many of our lectures there was invariably an old line medical professional who attacked what we were doing, reciting the old homily that a little knowledge about such complex and critical issues as medicine could be dangerous. To such criticisms we always replied by quoting T. H. Huxley: "If a little knowledge is dangerous, where is the man who has so much as to be out of danger?"

In spite of our critics, our efforts spurred on the imagination of a generation, giving impetus to the wellness movement we take so much for granted today. Less than five years following its debut, *The Well Body Book* was being ordered by doctors for their waiting rooms, and in many cases physicians were prescribing the books to their patients. In less than ten years, the book was being published in seven languages, selling a grand total of nearly a quarter-million copies.

As an author, I found numerous lessons in that experience. The primary one was that when Mike and I began to write the book we had no idea it would have such a powerful social impact. Moreover, there was something almost otherworldly about how the book was conceived. Many parts seemed to come from sources outside us, as if there was an invisible coach telling us what the world wanted at that time. If the truth must be known, we have both had trouble taking much credit for that book. We have always been aware that we were riding a wave that involved probably thousands of people, some of them ordinary people seeking a better way of caring for their health, others being doctors who knew there was something wrong about the high priest system that dominated modern medicine at the time. Mike and I were carried along on a wave far bigger than either of us or both of us together. What is undeniable is that the book made a big difference in people's lives, and we were privileged to be perhaps the equivalent of two tiny cells in the awakening of a new consciousness about personal health.

As a budding young author, I was mystified. This book had come out of a completely unexpected experience—a traffic accident. Yet, it was out of that ordeal that my passion for writing the book was born. During my college years I had read about the legendary muse that awakens the passions of poets. But if this was the sort of stimulus I required to write, I decided I'd better start looking for another line of work!

As I have worked with authors I've become as intrigued by the creative chemistry of the writer as I am with the act of writing itself. I find myself asking questions such as What are the deep inner resources from which successful authors draw? How do authors connect with that passion, bordering on obsession, that drives them to finish even the most ambitious writing projects in spite of seemingly insurmountable handicaps? How do we tap into and express the joys, sorrows, hopes, and fears that prod our readers to action or move them emotionally? What is the secret creative energy that the world's best writers can apparently zap into action the moment their fingers touch their keyboards? And what is it about the special bonds between author and reader that make writing as seductive, tempting, and irresistible as the most euphoric drug? I believe there are answers to these questions, some of them quite surprising, though I believe there are some essential secrets about language and writing that the universe will never disclose to us.

Not all the gifted writers I've had the privilege of knowing have been published. Many are not interested in doing so. Instead, they are members of a fast-growing fellowship who consider private journal writing to be an essential part of their spiritual and personal development. I have grown to have increasing respect for these men and women who, maybe even more than those of us interested in publishing, have discovered the real power of language as a vehicle to explore the inner space of human consciousness.

I have been truly blessed to be a witness to those extraordinary breakthrough moments in people's lives when, through their creativity, they come into their power as writers. Time and time again, as people read lines from a short story, poem, essay, or journal entry they had written, I have been spellbound watching the faces of the others as their hearts and minds, their very souls, were moved by the words. Although similarly moved by the words I am frequently awed by something more, something the readers may not yet know—that this breakthrough experience will change their lives forever.

My approach to writing, I'm afraid, has never been particularly literary. I have an idea this may have started as a reaction to graduating from a college creative writing program, where Literature, with a capital *L* was elevated to a golden pedestal, high up in the ivory tower. I always had the feeling that we were supposed to worship rather than have our lives transformed by the writings of people like Joseph Conrad, Dostoevsky, and even—yes, they definitely would have said "even"—John Steinbeck, who my teachers considered little more than a journalist with literary pretensions.

There was always the not-so-hidden message that high literature should be the goal of every graduate of the program, though try as we might we would probably never make it. Being far more proletarian than that, in my tastes as well as in my experiences as a reader, I constantly rebelled. In protest to one teacher's particularly stuffy approach to literature, I handed in a love story I'd written, about half of which consisted of a very graphic sex scene. I received a C-minus for my efforts, with a note scrawled in red pencil at the top: "We are not here to encourage young pornographers! Try to keep your literary efforts to a higher standard." I framed that page with its indignant scrawl and hung it on the wall behind my desk. It was a message to me that I should stick to a truth I'd first experienced as a child—that the real value of words for me was found in the delight of worlds they awakened in my consciousness, not in blind adoration or literary scholarship.

There are moments in all our lives so poignant, funny, tender, or perhaps even violent and heartbreaking that communicating them well transports both writer and reader out of their everyday view of the world, expanding their experience of life. Even more than from the great literary works, I remember scenes by my students. I recall the delicately drawn journal entry written by a young woman, telling of her first-time love, of a fumbling young man she loved very deeply but in her own clumsiness didn't know how to comfort and reassure when he couldn't consummate their passion. In this case, it was a true story about losing what is most precious in our lives because of the sheer bewilderment and embarrassment of our innocence. And I also remember the man—a cop with a poet's sensitivity—who read us a scene from his novel in progress describing an event he had witnessed during his years in Vietnam, when his best friend went berserk and opened fire on a mountain village, slaughtering dozens of women and children and turning what had been a pastoral setting into a bloody holocaust.

When the writer tells it from the soul, even the most gruesome, or embarrassing, or uplifting, or unconscionable, or even puzzling experiences can bring us closer, can remind us of our humanness and help us more deeply appreciate the gift of life. I tend to agree with Wallace Stevens, whose words I used at the beginning of this chapter, when he said that our role as writers is to help people—including ourselves, I would add—live their lives. I do believe that we fulfill ourselves when we can see our creations become the "light in the minds of others." What do we need to know to accomplish this? Unfortunately, there's not a simple answer. But the purpose of this book is to explore how to do that, to see and feel and hear and even taste what it's like when writers achieve it.

Language is one of those God-given gifts we often take so much for granted. We speak of people having good or poor communication skills, or we see language only as a way of conveying information. But I think it's much more. Perhaps there is a power greater than ourselves that gave us language so we could build bridges between our consciousnesses, allowing us to transcend the sense of separation we experience most of the time and so step, if only for brief instants, into our essential Oneness. Through words well crafted, like a superb bowl found in an archaeological dig, we provide evidence for the invisible inner worlds that make each of our lives unique while touching that ultimate point we all share with our hearts, making each strongly felt experience universal.

Through my writing, through the other writers with whom I've had the opportunity to work, and through the students who have taught me so much over the years, I feel as if I've become the custodian of certain insights about what makes good writing work. I believe that what this book offers is not techniques but a kind of cartography, a mapping out of the relatively unknown territory of the writer's mind. I offer these insights with a word of caution—that taking this information to heart, and really applying it in your writing, will change your life.

If you take your journey as a writer seriously, the end product is going to be much more than a published book, poem, article, or story, or a lifetime of personal journals. The path will take you beyond the surface of everyday life toward the inner space of human experience, where you cannot escape the awareness of creative sources far greater than yourself. You will discover, somewhere in infinitude of that seemingly private universe, heavenly bodies that we all see if we have the courage to look. When we're at our most impactful as writers, those bright stars of inner space shine through, inspiring awe and uplifting our hearts.

Even while extolling the powers of language in this way, I want to be careful I don't give the impression that our goal is to produce only "high literature." The greatness, if it does come across, comes because the author writes from his or her soul; it doesn't happen under the pretense of trying to impress the scholars. I have found as much uplifting and awe-inspiring passages in private journals as I have from the "great works" of the acknowledged masters. Similarly, being an avid mystery reader, I have found characters and situations from mystery books that have moved and even enlightened me as deeply as anything in Great Literature.

Rather, writing is a spiritual act because it invites us to look beyond the surface of life, to attempt to capture the essence of love, grief, joy, fear, compassion, pride, forgiveness, nobility, wretchedness—in short, the whole gamut of human existence. To write well we have to open to ourselves and to others. And as we'll be exploring in later chapters, language by its very nature does this, implying a sharing, an interchange between individuals that breaks through the barriers of our separateness. Why else invest all the energy that goes into learning to speak or write?

Without language we live in relative isolation, cut off from others of our species. That was the lesson in the biblical story of the Tower of Babel. The people of Shinar, who once spoke one language and had much power, attempted to build a tower with its top in heaven, so that they might be as gods and gain control of the entire world. To discourage their efforts, God confused their speech so that they would not understand one another. Without their common language their strength was negated because they could no longer coordinate their efforts to finish the tower.

Through the laws of language, we literally dissolve the distance between ourselves. We discover and share with others the uniqueness of our life experiences, and in doing so we discover the spiritual source that bonds us one to another. Presumably, we will not be punished for this—though one may be advised against challenging God's omnipotence by building a tower to reach the heavens!

3: A Place of Your Own

That inward eye
Which is the bliss of solitude.

WILLIAM WORDSWORTH

Early morning a day before my forty-second birthday, I put a change of clothes and a few extras into my backpack and lashed that, a small tent, and a sleeping bag onto the back of my motorcycle. Saying goodbye to my family and promising to be back in four days, I set out for the Gold Country, 150 miles east of my home.

As evening approached I made camp at Calaveras Big Trees, in a canyon called Squaw Hollow, three miles off State Highway Four. Eating tuna from a can, I lounged at the timber-heavy picnic table near my tent and realized I was probably one of the last campers of the season, at least until deer hunters came later that month, skulking into the woods with their guns.

I could smell rain in the distance; the sky was heavy, clouds iron gray, a chilling breeze. But I felt okay about the weather, slept well, and dreamed. Just before dawn I was awakened by a small black bear that blundered into the guyline of my tent. I stuck my head out between the tent flaps and stared eye to eye with it for a second, close enough for me to smell its fetid breath and see its long nose black and shiny. Then it fled, the fat under its shaggy black fur wobbling on its haunches, attesting to the fact that it had prepared itself well for winter, probably plumping herself up on stale donuts and watermelon rinds from garbage cans spilling over from tourists' refuse.

Late the next afternoon, I climbed to a ridge high above my camp; Thunder Hill to the north and McKee Hill farther east rose like magnificent grassy knolls, their rippling terrain carpeted with forests of spruce and fir. For two or three hours I climbed, exploring trails clogged with underbrush, barely passable. I moved cautiously, conscious of my path, avoiding fragile plants and wildflowers and passing a pair of grazing does that raised their heads only briefly, stared, chewing, a little annoyed by my intrusion.

I'd brought a camera along, and against the backdrop of dense forests I took pictures of a gray squirrel hunting nuts in the tall, dry weeds. The reddening evening light cast a smooth patina along golden stalks, the squirrel more silver than gray now, alert, tail curling along its back, head erect and swiveling, scanning the earth in short, quick jerks, searching for me, smelling danger. Undiscovered, I lay on my stomach, squinting through the viewfinder, proud of my craftiness, glad to go unnoticed. Through my camera's eye, a single weed, slender, golden, waving, bowed against the breeze, etched the sky, rare, alone, heavy with seeds.

Still later, I stood atop another ridge and watched the sun vanish, the glow over the forest soft and flat. For a while I saw seven horizons, seven receding planes of hills and trees, one behind another, like a stage set for a play. And because the sun was gone, the horizon began to turn gray, a black and white photo. The camera jiggled as I snapped the shutter.

It is still said that in the dark we see only in black and white, something to do with the nature of our eyes. So, imagining green more than seeing it, I felt an urge to return to my camp, maybe fearing the loss of color, a primal mystery reborn each night. In the distance I found the top of my tent through a clearing in the trees, its light blue geometry now gray . . . a few feet away the picnic table, black now . . . and the motorcycle leaning on its kick stand, crisp, manufactured, a foreigner in this ageless environment.

My camp looked comfortable, neat, inviting me. It felt good seeing it in the distance through the trees, and for a while I sat on the hill and enjoyed what I felt. The world took my silence for indifference, and in moments the treetops above me came alive. Squirrels worked the branches, pulling pine cones and breaking them apart for their nuts, then letting go, the cones crashing down through the solemn hearts of the trees, soft and final thuds signaling their arrival on earth.

At camp the mosquitoes were thick. I made a small fire in the circle of stones near my tent, the scent and smoke of the burning pine logs driving off the buzzing pests. Not wanting to cook, I sliced open a ripe avocado and ate it with a spoon. I also had a small chunk of cheddar cheese, some nuts and raisins, and a small bottle of cabernet I'd cooled under some rocks in the river fifty yards from camp. I ate slowly, sipping the wine, putting another log on the fire when the mosquitoes started again.

By the time I'd finished eating, it was dark. Wanting to write, I lit a small candle lantern and set it on the table. I could see my breath. The moon, bright, marbled the earth with shadows as its light filtered through the branches sheltering my camp. I shivered, finally got up and put on my riding jacket, then shivered again as I zippered it closed, the cool leather at first ungiving. But in a few moments the heat from my body, closed inside, warmed me, and the protective leather felt secure and known, moulding to my body the way it had done for more than a dozen years.

I wrote for more than an hour and thought there could be nothing better than to sit and write, alone in the darkness at a table in the forest. Later, maybe ten o'clock, I boiled some water on my campfire and made a cup of tea. I'd finished writing by then and had an urge for a cigarette or maybe a pipe of tobacco, though I hadn't smoked in years.

I heard footsteps on the gravel road that passed a few yards north of my campsite, then heard voices, a late-night conversation of two people who'd grown old together and knew what it took to gentle each other. I did not know where their camp was. I hadn't seen anyone else during the day, but there they were in the moonlight. Their voices came to me abstractedly, sounds that told me more than words would. I couldn't see their faces, but saw white hair and slender, straight, strong aging bodies that I was certain still embraced each others' youth. They passed and I was alone again, content.

The trees became bold black lines against the sky, silvered by a bright round moon and the Milky Way. Crickets chirped vaguely, their songs almost discouraged by the cold, replacing the day's last color with sound.

Fifteen years later I still call upon the memory of this and other periods of delicious solitude when the world around me seems too busy or demanding, resisting the peace the writer in me needs. I am not sure what it is in me that demands those slightly sad but settled and centered feelings that come with solitude, but whatever that state of mind is, it's a tremendously important part of the whole process. I find it impossible to write with another person in the room, and it's just as difficult for me to write outside, unless under the protection of towering trees or the darkness.

I am always amazed when people tell me that their favorite place to write is in a cafe or a public library. I remember one time walking into a small cafe in Santa Fe and noticing a young woman sitting alone at one of those tiny round tables, hardly big enough to hold her notebook, her paperback dictionary, and her *cafe latte*. In addition, k. d. Lang was singing "Constant Craving" in the background, and a thin blond man with a bright yellow T-shirt advertising Corona beer was shrieking into the receiver of the pay phone, letting the world know that he was enraged about somebody named Chris who had failed to show up for a date.

The woman kept her head down and her pen moving, apparently oblivious to what was happening around her. She had found her solitude, alone in a cafe, surrounded by strangers.

I'm not sure I've always recognized the importance of solitude, but now I know that it is essential to the creative process. Probably the first time I really became aware of the power of such moments was under the giant redwoods in Kings Canyon, at the southern entrance to Yosemite. I had driven up from Ventura, where I lived at the time, and had rented a small cabin for the week. With no electricity I wrote by the light of a kerosene lamp on a crude plank table. I put my words on a lined yellow legal pad, using my favorite fountain pen, a maroon Esterbrook with a gold-tipped nib that I had found in a secondhand store in Santa Barbara. The silence and the darkness under the trees was profound. Acutely aware of my senses in that natural sensory deprivation chamber, I wrote, "Nature is where there is no voice but the one you put there." The inner world from which I drew creative inspiration seemed to have been turned up a thousand decibels, with only the scent of redwood and molding leaves competing for my attention.

Many years later, while my family was still young, it became virtually impossible for me to find the kind of solitude I needed at home. I rented an office in town for a while, in a small building in Berkeley's warehouse district. But that didn't work. There was privacy, but there was also a constant buzzing of activity—of trucks going by, of the air conditioner humming, of phones ringing in other offices around me and above me. I certainly felt isolated and alone, but it was definitely not solitude.

One night I had a dream of writing in a tiny house at the back of a wild, unkempt garden. From the outside it looked like nothing more than a toolshed or a potting shed, but inside were bookshelves from floor to ceiling, a sleeping loft, and a built-in L-shaped desk with rows and rows of drawers that took up most of the floor space. If I sat in a mahogany swivel chair in the center of the room, virtually every drawer and bookshelf was within my reach. Two dormer windows let me look at tangles of wild roses—a profusion of subtle reds, pinks, and yellows—providing an illusion of space that was quite surprising. Outside, there were the roses, a small apple tree, and beyond that a flowering plum, resplendent with its outrageous pink blossoms. Inside, the entire space glowed with the warmth of dark, hand-finished wood.

When I woke the next morning I walked into our backyard and saw where the tiny building should go. The rest—the trees and flowers—were mostly in place. With a friend's help I built the structure in about two weeks, moved in my writing materials and books, and before the month came to an end was happily composing my next manuscript.

This was without a doubt my most perfect writing space. It contained me, like a womb, and in the security of those walls, with everything I needed at arm's length, my consciousness was free to roam. I wrote several books there over the next five years. When I moved on, that space was what I missed most.

However we define it, and however we get it, we need solitude. But I always remind myself that solitude is a state of mind, not a place. When we know what it is, what it looks like and feels like, we can create it for ourselves, almost—I say *almost*—regardless of where we happen to be. All writers discover how to get it for themselves, in time. For Hemingway, it was Paris, apparently the entire city, and after he had experienced it he had it for life. He said, "If you are lucky enough to have lived in Paris as a young man, then wherever you go for the rest of your life, it stays with you, for Paris is a movable feast."

Although solitude writers yearn for comes in different packages, it has some fairly universal characteristics. The most important one, I think, is a certain sense of safety—not safety from physical danger, such as getting struck by lightning or being abducted by space aliens, as much as a guarantee against insensitive interruptions. The creative process requires that we leave the external world and go into the inner one.

And while in that inner one, we don't want to be reminded of the external one. A telephone ringing, a spouse rushing into the room in search of car keys, a child shrieking in your ear demanding your attention—these interruptions jerk you out of the inner world, which is the life force of the writer. Although these sound like simple interruptions, to the person thoroughly immersed in the work of writing, they are assaults. Solitude nurtures us and respects the process we need to follow if we're to fulfill our dream.

I had believed that this nurturing place of safety we call solitude was an easy and natural thing, that everyone knew what it was and experienced it in their lives at least once in a while. Then, several years ago, I was asked by my friend Gabrielle Roth to address a workshop of about seventy people she was teaching in northern California. I was to spend three hours with each of four smaller segments of the larger group. As an introduction I guided them through a visualization exercise for creating a safe writing place, a place of solitude, an inner writing studio.

Halfway through the exercise somebody started sobbing. Then another person joined in, then another. When we'd completed the visualization, I asked people to share what their places of solitude looked and felt like. To my amazement, many people described these places with tears in their eyes, and even with much sobbing and grief. One woman in her early forties said that as I guided them through the exercise she suddenly realized that she had never had a space of her own. As a child she had shared a bedroom with her sister. In college she had roommates. While still in college she had married and shared her bedroom with her husband. She also realized that between raising her children, having a part-time job, and trying to be a good wife, she was rarely alone. The closest thing to solitude she'd ever enjoyed was in the bathroom taking a shower. Through the guided imagery exercise, she had created an imaginary place of solitude, which she called her "magical garden," where she could sit and meditate for hours or simply lie naked in the sun while butterflies and hummingbirds fluttered.

She was not alone. At least a half-dozen others shared the same mixture of sadness and joy at discovering the lack of solitude in their lives—sadness because they got in touch with something profound and rich that was missing from their lives, and joy because they had at last gotten in touch with what they'd been missing. The men in the class reported fewer problems with solitude. Most of them had not only experienced it many times, but they almost took it for granted, demanding and getting it from the world. Men reported experiencing it in sports, while running alone on a favorite trail, while working in a home workshop, while fishing, or even while driving to work in the morning.

The people who dream of writing but can't, who complain of "writer's block" or of simply being unable to begin, are the same ones who have no place of solitude in their lives. There's not a doubt in my mind that this is where good writing begins. I'm not saying it has to be in a rustic cabin under the redwoods or at a romantic cafe in Paris. But without some place to go, either in our minds or in our physical lives, where we can feel the luxury of solitude, the writer in us can never come out. I'm sure this is the place Wordsworth was talking about when he spoke of the "inward eye which is the bliss of solitude."

I used to do this long, meditative exercise in my classes, starting with a deep relaxation technique and then guiding people step by step into the mental imagery of an ideal writing place. And then I remembered: Good writing takes us there. That's what it's all about. So the ideal situation would be to give our writing a double purpose—taking us into the solitude, the ideal writing place, while actually getting some writing practice. The assignment turns out to be one of those pulling-yourself-up-by-your-bootstraps exercises. The writing puts you where you need to be to start writing, and you've actually started writing in the process.

One way is to work from memory. Go as far back as you want or need to get hold of your solitude. Or maybe you've had a relatively recent experience—even a fleeting moment—of solitude you'd like to work with. My best example was something a woman did in a workshop I gave in Ashland, Oregon. She was a runner, and some of her best but most fleeting moments of solitude came during her morning runs on a particular road in the hills. So she wrote about that. She wrote about the start of her run: the steep grade, the narrow, winding blacktop road, and the big dog that always charged against its chain in the front yard of a farmer's house and frightened her. It was a big black dog with a wide, thick jaw, and she was always afraid that one day it would break its chain, come after her, and tear her to pieces. But it never did, and every time she ran it was the same thing. A half-mile past the dog the road leveled out and she found her pace and it felt wonderful running on the dirt shoulder alongside the road, which was softer than the blacktop.

It was, of course, impossible to imagine how she could run and write, too. But she said that after a mile or so the running became automatic and she started writing in her mind. She was sometimes a million miles away, in faraway places she had visited or dreamed of visiting. She'd make up poems, and when she got back to her apartment in town she wrote down what she remembered. She said it was always the solitude of the run that got her into that place where her creativity took flight. Afterward, it was like taking dictation to get the words down because she had a very good memory, almost as good as having a tape recorder along.

If you can't recall moments of solitude, make them up. Where would you like to be? If you could have any writing studio you want, what would it look like? One man told about a beautiful cottage that clung to the side of the cliff overlooking the rocky coast near Big Sur, south of Carmel. Waves crashed under it, sending showers of sea water against its windows. In this imaginary writing place he had a servant who brought him meals—always perfectly prepared gourmet food—and a masseuse who arrived every afternoon to give him a massage so his shoulders wouldn't cramp up from sitting all morning at the word processor. Everyone in class loved the fantasy, though none of us knew a writer who could afford that kind of luxury life. But it didn't matter. The point is that in your mind you can have anything in the world you'll allow yourself to have. There are no limits.

Before you begin the following exercises, make a list of the five senses—sight, sound, touch, taste, and smell—and put it on the wall above your desk. Add emotion if you wish, but when you write always concentrate on what triggers those emotions, describing the triggers in terms of the senses. Now write a description of your place of solitude using plenty of sensory clues. Describe what you see—colors (the blue sky, the golden summer hills); smells (seaweed rotting in the sun); touch (sinking into the soft leather chair); temperature (shivering as you leaned over and touched a match to the neat little teepee of paper and kindling you'd set in the fireplace); sounds (a gentle breeze rustling the leaves of the oaks outside your window, the crickets chirpping); and mood (your sadness at parting slipping away and suddenly feeling strangely elated). Remember that the point is to put yourself into the scene. It's through describing what we perceive through our senses that gets us there and takes the reader with us.

If you have a good friend you can read to, read your description. If your writing carries your friend along with you, into your place of solitude, then you'll know you've succeeded. Having the experience of reading your writing to another person is tremendously important; we don't complete our writing until we've read it to someone else. Wherever we use language there's an implied reader. Even people like Emily Dickenson, famous for spiriting her poems away in a drawer so people wouldn't read them, knew that. She wrote: "A word is dead / When it is said, / Some say. / I say it just/ Begins to live / That day."

After you've written about your solitude and the place you associate with it, use it whenever you write. Remember that your greatest power as a writer, what you draw from for your inspiration, isn't *out there*, but inside you. Here's a line I always quote from Alfred North Whitehead: "The poets are entirely mistaken. They should address their lyrics to themselves, and should turn them into odes of self-congratulation on the excellency of the human mind. Nature is a dull affair, soundless, scentless, colorless; merely the hurrying of material, endlessly, meaninglessly."

It's not easy to remember that we are always, quite literally, making sense of our world. Nature doesn't have the scent of a rose; we make it up with the raw data we get from our senses, and then we mix it together with all sorts of associations that are stored in our brains. At best it's a kind of conspiracy between ourselves and what's out there, because we are, after all, as much creations of nature as are roses. I know that when I remember we are always projecting meaning to whatever is happening out there, and that there's really not much else any of us can do, it makes my work as a writer a little easier. Most of all, it reminds me that the most important and generous thing any of us has to give as a writer is our own voice, how we each experience our lives.

Maybe it's only in solitude that we can hear that voice clearly. And maybe that's as true for readers as it is for writers.

4: Is Anybody Out There?

'Tis the good reader that makes the good book;
in every book he finds passages which seem
confidences or asides hidden from all else and
unmistakably meant for his ear; the profit of
books is according to the sensibility of the reader;
the profoundest thought or passage sleeps as in a
mine, until it is discovered by an equal mind
and heart.

RALPH WALDO EMERSON

The first successful nonfiction book I wrote was about home schooling and setting up small private schools as an alternative to public education. The book came out of firsthand experiences, when we started sending our kids off to public schools. I discovered that there were many more parents than I would ever have dreamed who were dissatisfied or just plain angry at the way their kids were treated in school, but they did not know what to do instead.

In an effort to find some solutions, I started collecting information about taking our children out of public schools and starting schooling programs in our homes. I wrote a fifty-page booklet about it and sold it for a couple of dollars through ads in the classified sections of underground newspapers in the San Francisco Bay Area. I didn't sell a lot of them, but one day an editor from a small publishing company called and asked me a lot of questions about it. I told him all I knew; then he said he'd like to talk with me about writing a whole book on the subject.

His name was Don Gerrard. In the mid-sixties, before starting his publishing company (which would later become a Random House imprint) he was a book rep for one of the major publishers, traveling around northern California visiting bookstores and filling orders for the newest books. In his travels he had begun to notice a growing number of people publishing books and magazines out of their garages or kitchens, people doing some very exciting new work that the larger New York publishers didn't yet understand. Many of these publishing ventures were extremely successful, catering to that growing number of young men and women who were discontented with the way things were and wanted to make some changes. It was a whole counterculture changing society from the inside out.

Don had the foresight to recognize that this movement was something more than a passing fad—which was the way most East Coast publishers were choosing to look at it, a mistake that cost them millions of dollars worth of book sales each year. New York editors looked at the books published "out West" and invented a new term: "non-books," presumably because most of them were how-to or self-help books.

The problem for the new publishers was distribution; the alternative publishers could get their material written, printed, and bound, but they had only limited channels for getting their products to readers. Don took on several small publishers, selling their wares out of the trunk of his car while continuing to sell his regular line of New York-style books.

The business in alternative books grew at an astronomical rate. Seeing the writing on the wall, Don then started one of the first successful independent book distributors, Book People, which continues to be a strong and influential force in the book world today. After that, Don started Bookworks, his publishing company.

Don set up an evening appointment and gave me the address of his office in a rather seedy warehouse district of Berkeley. His well-lit office had an oriental carpet, a large wooden rocking chair, a big leather couch, and a bookshelf I later learned held copies of every independently published book he'd represented.

Don was in his early thirties then, a tall, good-looking man with a scruffy beard and a hint of a Texas accent. He apologized for not being able to offer me tea or coffee. He explained something about a small kitchen in the hallway that was locked at night.

He sat opposite me in the rocking chair while I lounged back on the couch. He flipped through some notes he'd made about my prospective book for a moment, then looked at the ceiling.

"Who do you think are your readers? Could you describe them?"

His questions took me off guard. I shrugged. "I suppose people like me, people who've had their kids in public school and maybe had a bad experience with it."

He nodded. "Your writing's okay. It's clear. You get the information down and all that, but then it doesn't go anyplace."

"It hopefully gets read," I answered, somewhat defensively. I really didn't get what he was driving at.

"Don't get me wrong," he said, apparently eager to keep me on his side. "I like what you're doing here. But when I sit down to read a book for myself, I look for certain things that I guess a lot of other people don't look for. And for better or for worse, that's what I try to publish. I like to publish books I want to read.

"I'm not necessarily talking about content," he said. "It's more a way of writing I'm looking for."

"A certain style, then?"

"I'm not sure I'd call it style. It's more an attitude, a way the writer has of acknowledging me, the reader."

I pondered this for a moment. "But that would require me to actually be there, to know the reader."

"In a sense, yes. I can't tell you how to do it, since I'm not a writer. But I know it when I see it, and I can tell you this much, it has partly to do with using personal pronouns—*I*, *me*, and *you*, mostly."

Don gave me some samples of writing that he liked, gleaned from several books. He told me to go home, look over the samples, and, using my material, try to write three or four pages as if I were writing a letter to a very good friend. He said after he'd seen what I could do we'd talk about the rest of the book and about his publishing it.

I went home and stayed awake until about three o'clock the next morning looking over what Don had given me and re-membering what he'd said. I definitely felt challenged. But I also felt angry and more than a little put down. I'd tried to im-press him with the fact that I was, after all, a *professional* writer, with three published books to my credit. Granted, they were children's stories for an educational publisher, but Don had not even acknowledged that much.

As morning approached I had a minor breakthough. It had to do with the quality of the writer's relationship with the reader. I realized that all my life I had resented people putting things out as gospel truth when it was only their opinion. This began for me in school but also had to do with writing. I remembered a history teacher I had in high school who epitomized this kind of behavior for me. Once I made the mistake of questioning him on a remark he'd made about the Pullman strike; he'd said that the strikers deserved being beaten and shot because they had acted illegally. When I foolishly asked him to explain this—I was a champion of the proletariat even then!—he snapped back, "It's true because I say it is, and if you want to get a passing grade in this class you'd better get that through your head."

The sample writing Don had given me to study was at the opposite pole. Even while presenting useful, relatively objective information there was a tone of humility about it that I found refreshing and supportive. It did, in fact, seem to acknowledge me, the reader, and in this acknowledgement it enlisted my interest. For example, three pages were from a book about building your own house. The writer had an entire chapter on what a first-time builder may be feeling—fears, how when you are learning to hit nails with a hammer you can't give up just because you bend a few or whack your thumbs a time or two. The writing convinced me of two things: first, that the author had been a beginner himself, and second, that he cared enough about me to share the difficulties he'd faced and overcome. Ultimately, the book was as much about human nature as it was about building a house.

The author took me by the hand and led me through the self-doubt, bruises, and blisters that I'd inevitably face if I were to take on this adventure. He also told me how to select lumber, frame a wall, put up dry wall, and more. But the human part really impressed me.

I was touched by the writing in a way I hadn't expected. I felt, this writer cares about me—or at least cares about people. He's taken the time to think about what it means to take in new information like this and attempt to apply it. He was the kind of teacher I had longed to have when I was growing up, somebody who could feel my frustration at trying new things and not being quite able to do them the first time around. He was the kind of person who appreciated what we all go through to move from ignorance to knowledge about a particular skill or subject. What showed through was his love for people, and in doing that he won my love.

As a reader, I wanted to know the author better. He literally lit up my life when he shared his own experiences with me. I loved finding out what he went through when he framed up his first wall only to discover he'd misread the blueprint and had cut fifteen studs the wrong length, the result being that he had to start over. The story told me that he was a human being just like I was, and if he could build a house—false starts, errors, and all—then I was pretty certain I could do the same.

So this was what Don had meant about acknowledging the reader!

The next morning I called in sick at work and locked myself in my study. I began rewriting my book about homeschooling. And what I quickly discovered was that the way of writing Don described was a perfect model for the kind of teaching I wanted to encourage in my book. I'd written my first draft in what I call a "Campbell's soup can" style, simple, straightforward, but without a personal voice. With the new way of writing, I now had a perfect marriage between form and function. I not only told my readers what to do to take their kids out of public school and educate them at home, but also I told them about my experiences with home-schooling. I told them what was scary about it and what they could do to handle the scariness.

I wrote about thirty pages during the next day and a half—cutting work for the rest of the week—and mailed them to Don. A few days later he telephoned to say how much he liked what I'd done. When I went back for our second meeting, we met at his home in north Berkeley. Since he was a counter-culture publisher, I was surprised to discover where he lived. It was a big, two-story place on a quiet street, with a small backyard and about six bedrooms. He lived there with his wife, Eugenia, three children, and—I learned later—almost always at least one house guest. By all outward appearances his lifestyle was very mid-American.

Don said he wanted Eugenia to sit in on our meeting because she was the mother of the three children who lived with them and thought we should know the perspective of a person who was a little nervous about going against convention. Eugenia had a long list of questions and concerns that she offered generously, which allowed us to flesh out the book so that even a person with many concerns about doing the right thing by their kids would have their questions addressed.

When I went home that night, I did so with a good book outline and a contract. When I prepared to write the next day, I also discovered something else: I now had an imaginary reader. Whenever I settled into writing, an image of Eugenia came to mind, sitting in the same room with me as big as life. Like a heroine in a favorite movie, she came alive for me, questioning, prodding, expressing her worries, then waiting for my replies. This was a new experience for me, and the more I worked with it, the more I liked it. My writing became more lively and colorful. It also became much clearer while providing a teaching model for my readers. The style I was evolving, out of the sheer desire to answer Eugenia's questions, was exactly the kind of teacher-student relationship I thought had to be developed if we were going to improve education in our country.

The more I wrote, the more I realized that by writing this way I no longer felt quite so lonely. One part of writing that causes most writers a lot of problems is that it is such a lonely profession. If you're to write, it means there's nobody looking over your shoulder to tell you what to do or when to do it. You have to do all that for yourself, although I suppose that in the same way you can create an imaginary reader, you can also create an imaginary boss to keep you on track with deadlines. (People often ask me how I discipline myself to write as many books as I have done over the years. I tell them that it isn't discipline at all; it's simple fear. I call it "keeping the wolf from the door.")

No More Public Schools was published six months later and sold more than thirty thousand copies during the next three years. It wasn't a best-seller, but its relative success encouraged me to quit my job and commit myself to writing full-time. During the next five years, I published three more books with Don and became his principal editor. I worked on several other authors' books with him, rewriting them when authors couldn't, or wouldn't, do the same.

I learned during those years that few people knew how to write in the personal style Don was honing in his publishing business. Some even resisted it. When we had editorial meetings with new writers, the subject always got around to writing experience. I remember one man we worked with, a health practitioner in his early fifties, who said that most of the writing he'd done was for school.

"You know," he explained, "in school they tell you to keep yourself out of the writing. Be objective. Back up anything you say with plenty of quotes from recognized experts in the field."

It was clear that a great big piece of writing instruction has been left out for most of us. Good writing for school almost always meant that you were supposed to keep your voice out of it. Mostly, teachers were interested in discovering whether or not you were paying attention, and how much or how little you had assimilated about what they'd tried to teach you. Personal opinions and firsthand experiences were not wanted, and if anyone had taught us about acknowledging the reader, I for one had completely missed it.

Oddly enough, for centuries we've known about the principle of considering the reader as a whole person. Sophocles talked a lot about it in the Poetics, though he was applying the principles mostly to theater. He talked about entertaining the audience, not only emotionally but intellectually, and that it was the ability to reach people in the audience and use their ability to laugh and cry, love and fear that made the difference between good writing and bad. Sophocles didn't know about writing nonfiction but the same principles apply. Good novelists know it, too: if they don't touch the reader's heart, the book isn't going to work.

I've worked with budding novelists and short-story writers, whose stories suddenly took on a new life, thanks to this simple insight about developing imaginary readers. When they finally did establish an imaginary reader, the characters in their stories came alive, too. "It's sometimes like working with a whole roomful of people," one writer told me. "Some of them get to be characters in my books, but there's at least one (the imaginary reader) who only I know about."

Even as I write these words, what comes to mind is that scene in the public library so many years ago, when I stood in front of a group of young people and, with knees shaking, read from my book. It was the first time I had experienced the role of the reader and the responsibility we have as authors to consider how readers are affected, or not affected, by what we say and how we say it.

One of my author friends once told me, "You have to fall in love with your readers. You have to realize that without their intellectual capacities, as well as their capacities to feel all the feelings you feel, you've got nothing to work with."

Writing is always a partnership between author and reader, then, and if you somehow miss that, your work will probably not be successful. This is not to say that you give readers what they want or expect. When you do that, you're no longer a writer, you're a hack. Hacks are like those infamous television producers who argue they "only give viewers what they want." In the first place, it's simply not true. They give viewers what they can most easily get their attention with—sex and violence. We're all hypnotized by scenes built around these subjects. And if we are mostly offered only such imagery, we quickly become addicted. For writers or television producers to argue that they're only giving us what we want is about the

same as the drug pusher who argues that he's giving his customers what they want. Neither group cares about the long-
term welfare of their customers, or the kinds of community
values their efforts are encouraging.

When we let ourselves love our readers, they know it. I
know it when I read something by an author who acknowl-
edges and respects me. A couple of summers ago, while teaching a workshop in southern Oregon, I asked people in the
class to write a twenty-minute description of their imaginary
readers. One man, Gil, finished in about ten minutes, then sat
back and waited for the others to finish. I was pretty certain
he hadn't written much. How wrong I was! When I asked for
volunteers to read, his hand was the first to shoot up.

He sat back and in a slow, quiet voice read his description.
His family was Mexican-American and they worked the big
farms throughout the United States. But mostly they were
based on a large farm in Texas. He told about his Tio Juan,
with whom he had a very special relationship. He described
one day in the field on a tractor, one of the giant John Deeres
used for plowing and pulling harrows to prepare the soil for
planting. Gil was a little boy then, about seven or eight, and he
was leaning against the fender as his uncle drove the tractor.
Gil wrote:

> My Tio Juan is my good listener. He takes his time and
> moves his soft brown eyes in my direction, tilting his head
> over to listen to me. We are on his tractor plowing a corn-
> field, and he stops the old John Deere to hear what I'm say-
> ing. He gives me his full grown-up attention. Taking off his
> straw hat he wipes his wide sweaty brow with the back of
> his hand. His eyes wrinkle up as he gives me a generous

smile. This big gentle man makes me feel completely safe, so I proceed to tell him just anything. He runs his fingers through his thinning hair. The hot Texas sun makes him squint, so he puts his well-worn hat back on. My sharing makes him laugh—like a kid himself—and then he says, "*No viejo, no tengas cuidado—yo te lo doy.*"*

As he finished reading Gil explained, "He always called me old man (*viejo*) a kind of tender term of endearment and respect. I don't know why. He always said I knew more than any child should know."

When Gil wrote, he wrote to his memory of Tio Juan. He wrote in gratitude for the love and respect this gentle, caring man gave the little child so many years ago. The tenderness and warmth in his writing touched the reader's soul so delicately and subtly, like a knowing look between lovers across the room—or maybe like a man stopping a big tractor in the middle of a hot Texas cornfield to hear what a child had to say.

As a reader I want to be entertained, edified, and informed. But I also want to feel that I know the author. Judging by the books that enjoy the biggest readerships, I'm not alone in this desire. In the sixties through the late seventies we changed a lot in our reading habits. Along with challenging people in power, like politicians, lawyers, manufacturers, doctors, and even educators, we started looking for a different way to measure trust. We no longer believed that if people had risen to positions of great power they were trustworthy. But if we couldn't determine trustworthiness according to their status in life or the little letters after their names or the schools they

---

*"Not to worry, old man, I'll take care of it" (translated for meaning and tone). This copyrighted material is used by permission of the author, Gil Campos.

went to what could we use to determine it? I know that the answer for me was how they came across to me as people. Why were they in medicine or politics? What did they get out of being top lawyers besides power and financial gain? If they could touch me on a human level, I was much more willing first to be drawn to them personally and second to begin listening very carefully to what they had to say. The one thing I could trust was personal truth—and this had something to do with how they felt about their work, how well integrated it was with the rest of their lives.

I'm not saying that everything is a matter of opinion or that only personal truth is important. I may like some people who perform brain surgery, but if they are going to saw a chunk out of my skull and fiddle with my gray matter, I also want to make certain they know their craft. Trust is personal, and personal isn't remotely possible until authors put themselves on the line and let you know who they are. And the person I trust is not necessarily going to be the one you trust. The bottom line, I suppose, is that particularly in writing there is no ultimate authority.

Writers, then, need to know how to talk to their readers. The imaginary reader is one of the best ways I know to do that, because having such a reader in mind as you write is a constant reminder that you are not doing all this work in a vacuum. At some point, if you do it well, your writing will be out there for thousands of people to read, and so, in a very real way, you connect with those readers across time and space. The imaginary reader is a conduit to them and as such it is as critical a part of the whole writing process as a telephone line or microwave broadcasting system is to communicating with friends across the country.

TO OUR READERS

When you develop an imaginary reader, do so with as much care as you'd take to develop a character for a novel or research the life of a major personality for a biography. Many people start with a person from their past or one who is in their life now, like Gil and his Uncle Juan. But even if it is somebody you're familiar with, take the time to use your writing skills to get them down on paper. To do this, make use of everything you've done up to now. Put yourself into your place of solitude, then focus on your list of senses so that you can describe what your imaginary reader looks like: What's the color of hair, eyes, skin? How old is this person? Where does he or she live? What's the living space look like? What's that person's relationship to you? How do you feel in the presence of this person? How does this person feel about you? What's this person's history?

My experience with creating an imaginary reader is that the more real I can make him or her, the more this person takes root in my unconscious. Even though you may never share with your readers the fact that you have an imaginary reader, there will be a big difference between the writing you do with one and the writing you do without one. And just because you're writing for yourself and will probably never share your imaginary reader with anyone else, don't be sloppy. You're the reader and the writer in this case, so make certain you respect both.

I'm not sure Ernest Hemingway had an imaginary reader, though I strongly suspect he did. Often his writing sounds like a postcard home, written to a friend he's known a long time. I've always believed his imaginary reader was the sister he talked about in his early Michigan stories, with whom he had a rather tender and protective relationship. He may not have been aware that he was writing to an imaginary reader, but there's such a strong sense of engagement between author and reader that I'm certain he was doing it on some level. Whatever the case, Hemingway knew the power of the author knowing things that were important to the story but not directly appearing in it. Once he said, "I always try to write on the principle of the iceberg. There is seven-eighths of it under water for every part that shows." The imaginary reader is in that seven-eighths.

It's best to write about your imaginary reader until he or she begins to take on a life of their own, the way a well-drawn character in a good novel does. After you've breathed life into your imaginary reader, you'll have a writing ally who'll be at your beck and call whenever you need them. Before you start to write, take whatever time you need to get that reader in focus. Then pretend you're talking to him or her. Ask for feedback: about the book idea, the plot, the way you composed the last paragraph or the last sentence. And then learn to listen for feedback. It will come if you give it time. So give it time.

Having an imaginary reader is different from what editors and writers mean when they talk about identifying your readership. Both are important, but the imaginary reader is usually much more personal, an ally you can consult with even about such matters as who your readership is. Identifying your readership can vary from book to book, depending on the kind of writer you are, and it's generally a much more logical process than creating an imaginary reader.

When you identify your readership, you're simply asking Who is this book for? What segment of the population might be interested in it? For example, the readership for this book is anybody who wants to become a writer or any writer who wants to hone his or her skills. If I use writing a book about personal health, my readership would be anybody concerned about maintaining health. The readership for a book about raising children with high self-esteem would be parents with young children or possibly parents who are contemplating having kids, and/or grandparents, educators, and social workers.

I cannot begin to tell you how many books I've seen get into trouble and not find their niche in the marketplace because their authors weren't clear about their readership. One in particular was a book about how our educational system fails to teach anything about financial well-being. Certainly this was an excellent issue. But throughout the book the author switched who he was talking to. Sometimes it was obvious he was addressing educators. Other times he was addressing parents with young children. Other times he was addressing people who wanted to know how to get rich. Reading it was like trying to look at a beautiful landscape through a telescope with a cloudy lens. By failing to sharpen his focus on one reader, the author didn't get any readers. The book could have sold more than 100,000 copies to any of those readership groups, but it sold less than a tenth of that total before it was taken out of print.

Sometimes, your imaginary reader and your focused readership are the same, and that will make your job a lot easier. I have a group of imaginary readers I consult. The one I used for this book is a composite of several people: my younger brother, who is already an excellent writer who occasionally publishes articles in fine woodworking magazines; a woman in her late forties who attended a workshop I taught and is working on what's going to be an excellent historical novel; and a cousin in Ohio who loves writing, but really has a struggle disciplining herself to do it. And, of course, I always include the publisher who bought my first nonfiction book, Don Gerrard. In addition, there are a couple of imaginary readers I don't share with the world; they demand anonymity.

Occasionally, people have trouble with another kind of imaginary reader—the inner critic. I'm sure all writers have inner critics but some of us have ones that are a lot tougher than others. In a few cases I've found that the inner critic is responsible for keeping some very talented writers from even beginning their projects. And there are others whose inner critics kept their writing styles so rigid and dull that nobody could read them; they opened up and were able to develop their writing only when they were finally able to make peace with those tyrannical critics. But that's the subject of the next chapter.

5: Making Peace with Your Inner Critic

It takes courage
to do what you want.

Other people
have a lot of plans for you.

Nobody wants you to do
what you want to do.

They want you to go on their trip,
but you can do what you want.

JOSEPH CAMPBELL

"Every time I sit down to write," Mark said, "there's this part of me that says, 'Who do you think you are! You're not a writer.' And then I get real defiant, like *I'm going to show him! I'm going to push on through it.* Then I get into this compulsive thing, what I call my *grunt mode,* where I start going back over my writing with a fine-toothed comb, making certain I've crossed every 'T' and dotted every 'I.' I keep going over every sentence to make certain there are no errors. It becomes almost a life and death issue with me, as if I have to make it perfect. I'm a great grammarian. I've got a dozen reference books telling me exactly how to construct a sentence. My spelling is perfect; it's my big guns against this inner voice that tells me I'm not a writer."

"I know that one," somebody else said. "But I have to confess I'm no grammarian."

"You're lucky," Mark continued. "Because I never get past the first page. I tear every sentence apart, naming every part of speech, even diagraming it sometimes. That's where the whole thing ends . . . with me obsessively pouring over the mechanics of every sentence, every paragraph. But no matter how many times I go over it, I always find something new to correct. Then I realize I'm banging my head against a stone wall, analyzing and rewriting and analyzing and rewriting all over again. Sometimes I never get more than a paragraph down, and finally I give up because no matter how hard I work at it, I can always find more mistakes or ways a sentence could be made better."

"Wasn't it D.H. Lawrence," a woman named Barbara said, "who talked about his coal-miner father who made fun of his literary ambitions, saying that he could never make an honest living that way, that it wasn't a manly thing to do? As I understand it, there was a part of Lawrence, even long after he had published many novels, that always felt that way and never quite felt comfortable writing, even though, on the other hand, he loved it. Sometimes I feel like that. I've written poems and short stories and even had a lot of them published. But every time I sit down to write, I can hear my father saying, 'For this your mother and I made all our sacrifices to send you to college!' The only time I feel halfway okay about what I do is when I get paid for an article, so that's why I write articles, I guess, and neglect my poetry."

The people talking were participants in early workshops I taught, when I introduced the imaginary reader material. To my astonishment and embarrassment, instead of coming up with supportive imaginery readers, about half the participants came up with severe inner critics, figures like strict and disapproving teachers or parents who still had a grip on them they weren't able to break.

In spite of my efforts to encourage them to put these harsh inner critics aside and create imaginary readers who would be understanding and supportive, there were always a couple of people in a workshop who just couldn't do it. Whenever they relaxed enough to get themselves into the mood to write, their harsh inner critics always butted in, rudely and aggressively, inhibiting all their creative efforts. If they were able to write at all, their work generally came out wooden and lifeless, boring to read, painfully stilted.

I always went home after those workshops convinced there were people whose inner critics were so fierce and tenacious that they'd never be able to write, their every creative effort squelched. It troubled me, partly because I knew I had an inner critic or two of my own who I suspected were making it tough for me at times.

The more I thought about it, the more upset and worried I felt, because I couldn't quite get a grasp of my inner critics. I knew some of them, had even learned to use them to my advantage in some cases. But when I tried to nail them down the way many people in my workshops were able to do, they eluded me at every turn. And then one night I had a vivid dream about my older brother, John, and I. As is my habit, I got up, stumbled into my writing studio, and turned on the word processor. When my dreams are that vivid, I like to write them down right away. The fresher they are, the better.

The dream involved running for political office with John, and I kept getting him mixed up with John F. Kennedy. At one point he'd be Kennedy, and at another time he'd be just my brother, John. Like Kennedy, he stood up in front of huge crowds and gave glorious speeches that brought hundreds of people to their feet, applauding. In the dream I sat on the stage beside the podium, watching the crowd and feeling very proud and awed by my brother's brilliance, privileged to be on the stage with him.

Near the end of the speech, having listed all his qualifications and the many contributions he'd already made to the community, he said, "Now, I'd like to make a surprise announcement." He turned and gestured for me to join him at the podium, then in a booming voice proclaimed, "I am announcing today that my brother Hal will be my running mate in the coming election."

At this point he turned the podium over to me. I knew I was supposed to make a speech, but I was totally unprepared. This whole thing was a complete surprise to me. I stared out at that sea of faces, eagerly looking up and waiting for me to speak. I froze. I opened my mouth but no words came. Horrified, I heard only a croaking sound over the public address system, a grotesque sound like something from a wounded animal. Faces in the crowd stared back at me quizzically, then turned to one another. Pandemonium spread through the audience as people fled from the room, pushing and shouting.

My brother shoved his way up to the podium and shouted for them to stop, to come back, but they didn't. That's where the dream ended, with my standing at the podium beside my brother, feeling completely frustrated, powerless, and humiliated.

As I finished recording the dream, I realized that it had a complement in real life. My therapist many years earlier had pointed out that I saw myself as insignificant next to brother John. I had learned early on that this was the safest role for me to play in the family. My parents idealized him, perhaps because he was born three years after doctors told my mother she could never have a baby. When John did come, they must have looked upon his birth as a miracle, the fulfillment of a dream they had thought would have to be abandoned. He was everything to them: precocious, strong, physically perfect, a darling baby, and a godsend. My coming, a year later, was almost anticlimactic if not bewildering to them. They never knew quite what to make of me. I was a complete surprise. So John easily maintained his already well-established role as the star of the family.

One day, when I was perhaps ten years old, I overheard my mother talking to my aunt. "Hal is our black sheep of the family. He came out of a very different mold than the rest of us." She laughed when she said it, but she also said it with such a degree of conviction that I knew she believed it was true.

At the time I didn't understand what she'd said, but what it meant became clearer and clearer every year. My therapist called it a self-fulfilling prophecy, which began with my parents simply being bewildered and surprised by my birth. From the moment I came into life I was cast in the role of the outsider—of a "different mold" than the rest of my family. Everything John was, I was not. He was looked upon as the great student and intellectual; I was seen as, well, certainly not much of a student and of questionable mental abilities.

He was the extrovert; I was the brooding introvert, prone to daydreaming instead of taking care of business in the real world. He went along with the program, doing his best to fulfill our parents' expectations for him; I rebelled.

I knew how to do one thing really well, and that was to support my brother in every way I could. Early on I had discovered that there was an invisible line I must never cross. I had to stay a step or two behind John in his shadow, applauding him whenever he did anything worthy. It was as if I were doing it less for him than for our parents, however. I sensed that it was absolutely essential never to bring into question even the slightest doubt that John was number one.

I did a pretty good job of fulfilling my assigned role in the family. But behind it all was terrible fear. I was on a dangerous mission, always one step away from an emotional disaster. If I made the mistake of taking that one step, I would topple into endless depths, lost forever. What made it worse was that there was an inner drive that was always tempting me to take that step, regardless of the consequences.

There were things I yearned to do but could not risk for fear that I would overshadow John. I loved working with my hands, doing artwork and writing. But I dared not commit myself fully to these activities because I feared that I might do something better than John did. So when I did them at all, I did them in secrecy, often destroying what I did or hiding them where nobody else would find them. It was a painful secrecy.

In the dream it was the same fear that choked off my voice, even when John invited me to share his glory. I had so thoroughly learned my lesson—what I must do to be valued and protected and loved within the family—that even when the opportunity was handed to me I could not step forward. I couldn't make use of the opportunity because by speaking up I risked challenging my parents' perceptions of John's and my identities.

What the dream told me was that most of us have inner critics, and that they can exert an extremely powerful influence on our creative lives. Furthermore, they can have many faces and are often just one part of a family emotional dynamic that has many interlocking pieces. In my case there was a trade-off—what my therapist called a secondary gain—about standing in my brother's shadow. I was trading the obvious gain for a less obvious one. In fact, I sometimes wonder if it wasn't all secondary gain, because there was very little primary satisfaction in being dumber, less talented, and less handsome than John. I reined myself in and made myself virtually invisible so that my parents could feel safe in their illusions about him. The things children ordinarily do to win their parents' love, that is, doing the very best they could with the talents they had, were taboo for me. Holding back my talents was the way I won their love. The only way I could feel valued in the family was to be less than I could be.

My therapist told me that that did not mean I was doomed forever to hold back. On the contrary, she said, we often find our greatest abilities by looking more closely at the early patterns in our lives and then transforming them. She was a clever counselor. As we worked together I came to the conclusion that I could take advantage of my early teachings by serving others who, like my brother, were "stars" of the family, in this case, stars of the larger family to which I'd become attached in adulthood.

In the early sixties I discovered I was good at working with other writers, and I enjoyed working with them. Mostly the authors I worked with were high profile lecturers or workshop teachers. Publishers wanted books from them because they were highly visible and their visibility helped to sell books. But these people often didn't have either the time or the ability to write books. That's where I came in. I quickly learned that I could work with them the same way that I'd worked with my brother in my childhood. I learned to study their communication styles and write in their voices. I was so good at it that many stars I worked with couldn't distinguish between my writing and theirs. But because they couldn't I became virtually invisible to them. Ironically, the very talent that made me valuable to them also made it extremely difficult for them to recognize my contribution. My efforts usually went unrewarded—except financially. I began to make a good living.

I took great pride in my invisibility. If I had an ego investment in my work, it was in being able to give people exactly what they wanted. I sometimes saw my role as something like an actor, playing out other people's scripts, making their work look as good as I could make it look, but always hiding who I really was. Publishers loved me and rewarded me well for my efforts.

Writing alone, writing my books, was always a painful process. Even today, as I write these words, there's a level of anxiety, a sense that I'm risking much, that there is danger in putting myself on the line. But the more conscious I've become of my inner critics and the more clearly I've been able to see them, the easier it has become to work with my craziness.

I see and hear my inner critics in the background. They don't exactly tell me "Don't do this." They only look pained and bewildered when I speak from my heart. There's a part of me that goes forward and does it anyway, in spite of feeling anxious about hurting them.

I often think that creativity is a lot like intuition in that it's something we are born with, something that's always there right under our noses. Learning to tap its many riches isn't a matter of learning as much as it's a matter of *unlearning*. I have an inner guide, a native American figure, a toolmaker I call Awahakeewah. Some years ago I was in crisis. I had a major dose of that dread disease they call writers' block. Whenever I decided to write, I totally drew a blank. It was as if I had lost my ability even to think.

On one particularly gloomy day, I did the only constructive thing I could do under the circumstances; I put on my earphones, listened to a quiet environmental tape of ocean waves lapping gently against the shore, and meditated. The sound of lapping waves drowned out the background noise of traffic and ringing phones in my office—which was on a busy street in Palo Alto at the time—and after a half-hour or so, Awahakeewah began to come forward in my consciousness.

"What's going on with me?" I asked.

He smiled gently, understandingly. "You must understand," he said, "your creativity does not belong to you. It is part of the Creative Spirit that makes us all, that gives us life and that gives the entire universe its form. You have been given your small share of the Creative Spirit, but you are treating it as if you owned it. It is not yours to own. So get the hell out of its way!"

This conversation seemed so real to me, and so unexpected, that I suddenly popped out of the deep meditative state I'd sunk into and asked myself aloud, "How am I standing in its way?"

The answer didn't come immediately. But something was knocked loose and within an hour or two, I began writing. The ideas and words came quickly and easily, flowing onto the paper effortlessly. At the time I was working on a book for another person, but a project of my own, which I'd been struggling with for more than a year, made its first stirrings and broke through.

Remembering Awahakeewah's counsel, I remind myself that our own creativity is a sacred trust. If we are blocking it, consciously or unconsciously, through the inner critic or any other psychological impediment we're using, it's almost as if we're committing a kind of sin. My guide's teaching is that we are never more generous, never more blessed, than when we give of ourselves through that little piece of the Creative Spirit that lives in each of us. Letting our inner critics stand in the way is self-indulgent, maybe even narcissistic.

I may never be completely free of my inner critic—of the dynamic that tells me my only value is through serving others—but in so many ways it has been one of my greatest teachers. And I think that maybe this is the way it is for all of us. We can't deny our critics. We can't pretend they're not there and push them away, hoping to replace them with ideal imaginary readers. I believe they live on within our inner worlds, and as we get to know them better we can march them out and make them characters in our personal stories. In doing so we take one or two steps back and allow them to grow, to reveal to us the fears and misunderstandings that make them want to act as they do.

I still hold those parents who were so afraid I'd step out of my brother's shadow in my inner world. But I've given them permission to come alive. I've let them become the rich characters, like the characters in a good novel, who have lives separate from mine. I no longer see them just from the perspective of how they've made my creative life difficult. I see my mother—the inner one—in her childhood, wanting so much to idealize her father, to hold him high in spite of knowing a dark secret that shattered her image of him whenever she let it through. And I see my inner father resentful of his parents, angry at his father for dying too soon. My inner father, like me, served his brother, putting him through medical school to fulfill his mother's dream. Both my parents clung to their fears, embracing them, and in doing so they held back the truth that would have set them free.

I play with their fears in my mind, seeing through them, feeling their grief and their bewilderment, putting it down on paper, in my journals and, sometimes, in stories I write. The richer and more real they become in my mind, the more I feel free of them. It has become a strange kind of co-creative process, living with each other in the service of a power greater than all of us put together.

I don't believe the path to freedom, and to our greatest gifts, is found by complaining and bemoaning our battles with the demons we call our inner critics; rather, we find freedom by transforming them and making them into our teachers. Our inner critics are the known paths of our lives, and as much as we may hate them and feel ourselves limited by them, we cling to them because they are familiar. We jump into the un-known when we dare to make them more real, not less, and it's then that we abandon the familiar path and go out on our own, fully embracing our creativity. We can do so by letting these characters have their own lives, separate from us, and then choosing to—as Joseph Campbell so often advised—break out and "follow your bliss pattern, quitting the old place, starting your hero journey, following your bliss."

6: Coming to Your Senses

How good is man's life, the mere living! how
fit to employ
All the heart and the soul and the senses
forever in joy!

ROBERT BROWNING

The phrase "windows to the soul" sticks in my mind at this moment. My impression is that I've heard those words repeated in a hundred love poems. Maybe not. At the same time, I don't believe I'm being original when I think of the five senses as the way into that most elusive inner core of our being.

Does the soul really give a damn about the orange hues of a desert sunset or the crystalline, luminescent moon hovering over a snow-capped mountain peak? Apparently it does. When I think back to the truly special moments in my life, I immediately recall a wondrous concert of the senses when I was a child—the soft hush, hush, hush of gentle waves lapping against the shore on Lake Michigan, the cry of a gull hanging on the wind, white wings tipping against a flawless blue sky. And many years later, I recall lying with my lover, our sleeping bags rolled next to a lush green meadow high in the Sierras, gazing into the infinitude of the heavens dotted with brilliant specks of silver, a chorus of coyotes telegraphing their lonely songs across the miles. What lures me back to the deep satisfaction of such moments is the color, the sound, the scents, the sweet subtle touch of a warm breeze on my skin.

I've often thought how paradoxical it is that our spirits leap to the delight of the senses. It's ironical to think that the soul, which is not supposed to be tempted by the delights of the physical body, would find such pleasure in the senses. I can't help but wonder if the religious moralists who teach the piety of the soul haven't deliberately misled us.

This morning before I began to write, I turned to some pages in a journal from several years ago. The entry that caught my eye described a pow-wow I'd attended on the Stanford University campus. Each year native Americans from throughout the United States go to Stanford to celebrate. That day I stood at the edge of the football field watching the dancers. Native Americans from a dozen nations, many of them dressed in traditional costumes, moved in a dusty circle around the track at the edge of the field. It was a blazingly hot day; the sun burned on the dancers, who appeared to bask in its rays. Flashes of brightly dyed fabric, red and turquoise and yellow and green, swept by as the dancers flowed past, following the rhythm of drums whose reverberations filled the air, vibrating even the ground under our feet, like the heartbeat of Mother Earth herself. Many dancers wore anklets, each with as many as a dozen small brass bells, that jingled in a magnificently clangorous chorus with each step, the sound mingling with the steady life-giving beat of the drums.

I watched the dancers' feet as they moved in an endless circle around the field and realized they were doing something very different from what I had thought. Each step was deliberate and purposeful, yet almost a shuffle, as if to caress Mother Earth and to feel her skin, to sense her life, her spirit. It suddenly became clear to me that their movements were not intended as an exhibition, as I'd thought, but as a way of experiencing something I could not see. The dance was about touching the earth, letting her know we are here, feeling her under us as a live being whose support and love we must celebrate.

Here, all the senses—sight, sound, touch, smell, taste— came alive, the colorful costumes, the cacophony of the jingling anklets, the reverberating heartbeat of the drums, the whoops and cries of the dancers, the air rich with the aromas of burning sage, sizzling fry bread, lamb stew bubbling in huge pots, and the sweating bodies of the dancers in the summer heat. What I'd give to make a page of type do all that!

Words want to rest on the page much more quietly. The little black squiggles on a white field would prefer just to lie there, abstract and frozen in time. Yet, when I read words associated with the senses, like *red, blue, green, jingling, thumping, sour, sweet, velvety, soft,* or *a sensuous breeze over the skin,* something is excited deep inside me. When I recall the jangling clamor of a dozen prancing dancers, each wearing anklets of tiny brass bells, I am transported out of my everyday thoughts. How is it that the mere mention of color or sound, smell, taste, or touch awakens a sense of deeper involvement? What are the inner doors our senses open to us? Because with these doors flung open, we invariably step over the threshold, crossing the boundary that previously separated author and reader. We are taken into the other's life, and in the crossing we relinquish our own boundaries.

Back in my college days, I had a friend who was blind. Something happened during Jerold's birth so that he could see nothing but a slight sensation of light. He said he could tell if a room was dark or light, but that was about all. But in spite of his blindness, he wrote poetry with rich, dramatic imagery.

One day we were walking across campus. When we walked together he always folded his white cane, which telescoped so that it fit in a little leather holster on his belt. He walked close beside me, not quite touching, and no matter how fast I walked he kept up, striding along as if he had perfect sight. He explained that he had learned how to jog with a friend who was sighted. They'd worked it out so that his friend sort of "drove" him, taking into account the space Jerold would require to turn a corner, in the same way you take into account the size of a car when you're behind the wheel. He said it was easy to sense the energy of the other person and move in concert with it, as long as he was no more than three or four feet away. He liked walking fast beside me and not being cautious the way he had to be with the cane.

I asked him one time how he could create such coherent imagery in his poetry, because he had never been able to see. He shrugged.

"Partly from the feel of things. Partly from other clues— sound, for example. I tell a lot from sound."

"In your poems you always describe colors," I said. "How can you do that if you've never seen color?"

"Seen it?" he asked, obviously somewhat surprised by my question. "Do you think a person depends on his eyes to see color?"

"I would think so," I said.

"Don't you dream in color?" he asked.

"Sure."

"Maybe it's like that. After all, where are your eyes in a dream?"

"I would have a memory of color," I argued, "since I walk around every day with eyes that see. But where would you get the information to know these things?"

"I can't explain it," he admitted. "Maybe the green I see is different than the green you see. I don't know. How would you tell?"

We played a word association game then. I would say a word and he would say the first color that came into his mind. I'd say "grass"; he'd reply "green." I'd say "car"; he'd reply "could be any color." I'd say "anger"; he'd reply "red." I'd say "placid, calm"; he'd say "blue, sometimes dark blue, sometimes very light blue." I'd say "sun"; he'd say "yellow, maybe orangish red."

Then we switched. I'd name a color; he'd say the first word that came into his mind. I'd say "red"; he'd say "excitement, danger, stop." I'd say "green"; he'd say "landscape, peacefulness, vegetation."

Neither of us ever quite solved the puzzle, but something became clear to me from that exchange: There is a part of us beyond the physical senses that responds to suggestions of touch, taste, smell, sight, and sound. Jerold pointed out that Helen Keller, who was born without the ability either to hear or see, nevertheless found great pleasure in all the senses through her reading and writing. She once said, "Literature is my utopia. Here I am not disfranchised. No barrier of the senses shuts me out from the sweet, gracious discourse of my book friends."

My wife and I have two small dogs, each weighing about six pounds full grown. Every morning we take them for a long walk on a trail beside an estuary near our home. Although they were originally developed as lap dogs, ours have apparently never read the breeders' manuals because they love nothing better than running free in the great outdoors. We take them to the trail head in the car, and when we are near where we let them out, they start howling with excitement, crying to get out and run.

Today when I took them out, it was 6:30 in the morning. Cicely, the older of the two dogs, leapt from the car and raced down the short hill to the water's edge just in time to nearly collide with a magnificent blue heron rising from the edge of the bank. The bird spread its splendid five-foot wingspan and lifted high in the air, the dog craning her neck to watch, eyes wide with amazement, her entire body trembling with awe. When the bird was fully airborne the dog turned and ran back up the hill to meet me, jumping up on my leg as if to get my attention, to make certain I'd seen what she'd just seen, then running down the hill at breakneck speed, nose to the ground, racing in the direction the bird had flown. Maddy, the puppy, followed after her, her short feet barely skimming the ground as she almost took flight herself.

I followed the dogs, who quickly gave up trying to catch the bird who'd settled on the water several hundred yards ahead of us. The two dogs ran back and forth across the trail, noses to the ground, stopping every few minutes to investigate a scent more thoroughly, frequently marking that spot with their urine. Their delight with this world of scent was expressed in their frolicking movements. Their ears pricked up, alert, their bushy white tails waving wildly back and forth, held high; they were rapturous, jubilant, their souls singing.

As I followed them, my spirits soared. Watching them ca-
vort, exploring this world of scent, I could not help but wonder what it was they were finding so delightful. The smells
that delighted them were nonexistent for me, and when I let
my imagination entertain the possibilities, I must confess that
I was grateful. I have an idea I might not have been able to
share their fascination with those perfumes. Even so, the
scents obviously spoke to something that lifted those small animals' souls and in the process lifted mine.

Whatever it is that delights us about the senses, be it the
mysterious smells that elude me even as they enchant my
dogs, or the sounds of music that raise my spirits but leave my
animals cold, is a great mystery to me. By all rights it does not
seem feasible that the evocation of the senses would open the
doors to the soul. Even more a contradiction is the notion that
words could set the whole thing in motion and even at times
fill the darkness with light and color or the silence with voices
and song.

Assuming it's true that our real identity is spiritual, and
that we've taken a physical form in order to learn certain
lessons, I'd like to suggest that the puzzles we're here to pon-
der may ultimately be revealed through the senses. And
maybe we've been given language to push the riddle to an
even higher level of implausibility, where we are willing to say,
after all, that the universe is truly beyond our finite capacities.
If we play with language and the senses long enough, we will
be led to the soul where we can finally say "I don't know" and
be completely at peace with that.

7: Our Search for the Elusive Present

To observe without distortion is only possible if there is complete attention with your body, your nerves, your mind, your heart, your ears. Then you will see, if you so attend, that there is no entity or being called the observer. Then there is only attention.

J. KRISHNAMURTI

Occasionally I'll find a quiet corner in a coffee shop or other public place where I can write. There is one such place near my home, a cafe at a small lake near the center of what locals call Shoreline Park. It's a grassy park in the middle of a wetlands preserve of several thousand acres on the edge of San Francisco Bay. You can't swim in the lake, but it is a good place to sail small boats because from one o'clock until dusk there's a strong steady wind that comes in over the bay. In the summer months, with school out, the lake attracts throngs of windsurfers and young sailors who like the relative security and shelter it provides.

I've always been envious of those people who can take a pad of paper and a pen and write for hours in public places, but like the sailors on this little lake, I seem to need boundaries, a container.

One day I sat outdoors at the cafe. It was pleasant enough to feel the heat of the sun on my face and the wind in my hair, but I felt frustrated because I couldn't get into the writing I'd planned. I had the sense that my thoughts were soaring beyond my reach and I couldn't lure them in with my pen. If I only had four walls around me and a roof over my head they couldn't escape.

Across the patio on my left was a young couple leaning toward each other over the table. He was sitting with his back to me, wearing a blue blazer and neatly pressed white trousers, both of which seemed out of place in the summer heat. She was in a two-piece swim suit. I could see only her bare right shoulder and part of her right leg, the rest blocked by her companion and by a white plastic chair in my line of sight. I could see that their hands were resting on the table close enough to touch, but they were not touching. It was impossible to determine their mood from where I sat, but my impression was that there was a great chasm between them that yearned to be bridged.

I watched them for several minutes, looking for clues about what might be going on. Then I heard a shout of alarm. I turned to my right in time to see a barefoot toddler, dressed only in diapers, running toward the lake, with a young blond woman in jeans and a red sweatshirt in hot pursuit. There was a five-foot gravel strip just before the water's edge, and as the child reached it she lost her balance, tried to recover, then hurtled forward. A second later she tumbled face first into the water. The young woman scooped her up, lifted her high, and spun her around, laughing, then came galloping back up to the patio where an older woman was standing stiffly, shaking her head and scolding.

The young woman was taking the whole incident very calmly, even making light of it. She held the little girl in her arms and sat at one of the tables. The older woman sat opposite her, and even from fifty feet away I could hear them arguing. The younger woman was getting a thorough scolding and the child, who hadn't been upset, began to cry, clinging to the woman's bosom and hiding her face from the older woman.

When I turned back to the young couple, I discovered they were gone. Although I looked around, I could see no sign of them. I was curious about how they could have disappeared so fast. But in an instant I had almost forgotten about them.

One small sailboat was in the middle of the lake, moving away from me. Its gray hull was heeled over at a forty-five degree angle, and the sailer was leaning out on the starboard side, counterbalancing against the wind. He drove the boat hard; waves lapped over the gunwales, threatening to swamp the hull. But he went on, coming about only when he had run out of lake, about a half-mile away.

There is a peculiar kind of privacy I experience in public places. Being among strangers, I retreat into myself. If I pay close attention, it is easy to see how much I project to the world. I try to quiet my mind, to stop projecting meanings that aren't there, to be more attentive to what's going on around me, and for short periods I lose myself completely in the scene. Like in the Krishnamurti passage at the beginning of this chapter, there ceases to be an observer. I feel myself merge with the landscape, with the activity going on around me.

The trouble is, I can't write in this frame of mind. To write one has to become a writer—that is, an observer—and this means stepping back, moving just outside the scene. The best I can do is be an observer observing myself sitting in this moulded white plastic chair, at this round moulded plastic table, watching the sailboat on the lake now heading back in my direction. I am the observer who watches me sitting there, linked to others around me by little more than proximity—the sailer in his boat on the lake, the two women and the child, the man in the blue blazer and the woman in the swimming suit who are no longer here. It's odd how the observer part allows me to merge with the landscape, even lose myself in it, yet be there to notice, to take notes.

I have an idea that writers, more than most, know the observer self. I'm not sure how it is for other writers, but at times it is as if my everyday self, the self that takes part in the always-unfolding drama of life, is simply in the service of the observer self. Or is it vice versa? Perhaps it's the everyday self that wonders about the man in the blue blazer whose hands don't reach out to touch the hands of the woman opposite him. It's the everyday self that reacts with alarm as the toddler loses her balance and plunges head first in the lake. It's the everyday self that feels what it must be like to be a sailer hanging far out over the gunwales of a sailboat heeling sharply in the wind. And without the self that stands outside the scene, could we write at all?

Writing in public places reminds me of the partnership between these two parts of myself—experiencer and observer, if you will. The experiencer self has the strong awareness of possessing a physical body that separates me from the rest of the world. It's the self that owns the senses through which I become aware of sounds and shapes and smells and scents and texture and movements around me. It's the self that owns the personal history that causes me to fear, celebrate, wonder, or feel conflict about events around me. The observer self is, as far as I can tell, passionless.

Most writers I've known have had a difficult time balancing these selves. I remember reading an essay by Henri Bergson, the French philosopher and literary critic, who talked about the powers of the observer self, about there being a fine line between tragedy or pathos and comedy, and that all we needed to do to transform pathos or tragedy into comedy was to step back into the observer viewpoint. In doing so, we no longer had an emotional investment in the scene. We could smile and let it go because as long as we remain in the observer frame of mind, nobody gets hurt. Life is seen only as an illusion, where the passions that seem so earthshaking to us from our everyday perspective become absurdities.

Immersed in the landscape, lost in the passions of our lives, any sense of separation, or of being able to step outside ourselves, fades. Writing alone in a public place, where the passions of life are happening to other people as they might happen on a stage, I become a voyeur who never gets too deeply involved. My observer self dominates at such moments. And if I respond with alarm or curiosity or any of the other reactions to our lives, my observer self intrudes with its timeless detachment, its jaded, philosophical indifference reminding me that all is vanity.

The observer self is invaluable when we want to immerse ourselves in a scene and bring the present alive in our reader's mind. It stands outside us, like a lifeguard ready to dive in and drag us out if it looks like we're going down. And it may be this part of us that guards over the craft of writing itself, reminding us that it is only the artful rendering of the raw material of life that elevates our writing above gossip or telling jokes over a few beers. It's the craft that makes the ordinary universal.

In spite of its disdain for the senses and for what it considers human shortcomings, my observer self is always reminding me of the quest for the present. Like Krishnamurti, it reminds me constantly that our greatest power lies in our ability to observe without distortion. This is achieved by giving complete attention to our bodies, our nerves, our minds, our hearts, and our senses. And ironically, when we give such attention, that's when the observer vanishes.

It is the greatest of all life's contradictions, perhaps: when we are most focused on our physical being is when we see beyond it into the nonphysical, the timeless, the universal. What's more, it is from this presence of mind and body that our words best communicate to others. Just as deep meditation takes us to the place where the observer self dissolves, so the boundaries between reader and writer are dissolved when the latter is able to help the former focus on the present, on the senses, and on what we are holding in our hearts and minds at the moment.

Language isn't the best way to accomplish this, however. Especially in English we're constantly forced to use the past tense: "I *was* walking down the street smelling the flowers." It begins to sound contrived if we say it in the present: "I *am* walking down the street smelling the flowers." The illusion doesn't work. As you read this sentence, you know I'm not doing what I'm saying. So you're not taken in. The conclusion is that under the best of circumstances, we writers must create our illusions in the past tense.

Years ago, a novelist I studied with described a trick he'd learned for breaking through writer's block. The trick was to start writing about exactly what was happening in the present. He said to be as sharply focused and attentive to the present as possible. It might go something like this:

> I am sitting in front of my computer screen, my fingers moving over the keyboard. As they move they make funny little clicking sounds, dull rattles I find comforting. With each finger motion a new letter appears on the screen. Letters become words and words become whole paragraphs. The telephone rings to my left and I resist the pull to answer it. I stop typing as it rings and rings, ten times in all before it stops. I put my hands back on the keyboard but then I start to worry. Who could be calling? What was so urgent to ring ten times?

Although this is a most mundane activity, describing it brings me into the present. I immediately calm down. All the words and images and ideas that normally bounce around in my mind slow down. I become increasingly attentive to my senses, my body, my mind. Oddly enough, when I've accomplished what I set out to do, the reader is then transported into my world. Together we enter the illusion of moving more and more into the center. Just as in meditation, we stop watching ourselves living our lives and *become* life.

All the great sages seem to profess the same concept, from Mohammed and Moses to contemporary thinkers like J. Krishnamurti, Abraham Maslow, and Joseph Campbell: To thine own self be true. Follow your bliss! The way to that self, that bliss, is always through attentiveness to the present. Why it happens is still a mystery to me. But each time it happens, each time I accidentally or deliberately bring my attention fully into the present, whether on the page or in real life, I am once again sold on the idea. And if too long a time elapses between experiences of such moments, I recite to myself some lines by one of my favorite poets, Wallace Stevens:

> Just as my fingers on these keys
> Make music, so the self-same sounds
> On my spirit make a music, too.

8: Higher Creativity and the Peak Experience

All other memories of travels, people and my surroundings have paled beside these interior happenings. . . . but my encounters with the "other" reality, my bouts with the unconscious, are indelibly engraved upon my memory. In that realm there has always been wealth in abundance, and everything else has lost importance by comparison.

C. G. JUNG

Last night I awakened from a dream and for a long time lay in bed luxuriating under the warmth of the soft down comforter, trying to remember it all. In the dream it was a crisp fall evening. I was standing on a dock made of weathered planks as thick as railroad ties. It stretched out a hundred feet into a deep blue lake a half-mile across and two miles long. I looked over the water to the opposite shore and a dense green wall of cedars. The sun dropping below the hills behind me made shadows quickly spread through the trees. There was a mystical quality about the landscape, as if it had been drawn not from nature but from an artist's rendition of a lake. The colors were too intense for a real landscape, and the entire scene appeared as if frozen in time.

I was there alone, and I had the clear sense that I was no more than ten or twelve years old. I walked onto the dock and knelt to untie a rope wrapped around a chock fastened to one of the planks. I dropped the rope into the bottom of a wooden rowboat bobbing a few feet below me alongside the dock. Then I slipped over the side into the boat. As it took my weight, the boat tipped slightly. I adjusted my weight, took a step toward the center seat, and sat. I shoved away from the dock, swinging the bow toward the middle of the lake, then took the oars, lifted them, dipped them into the water, and pulled, and the boat slipped forward away from the shore.

I rowed toward the center of the lake, dipping the oars, pulling, lifting them, leaning forward, dipping, and pulling over and over. The boat moved effortlessly over the water. I rowed until I could no longer see the dock. Each time I pulled the oars, the boat rose then fell on gentle waves. The rhythm of my rowing joined with the rhythm of the waves, rocking my body sensuously, sublimely. I could no longer see the shore or the sky. I saw only the water around me and the worn gray gunwales of the boat on either side of me. I saw the bottom of the boat, narrow planks damp from the water that dripped from the oars as I rowed.

As I moved across the lake, something very odd began to happen. I was no longer just the boy in the rowboat. I was also the boat and the lake and the sky. I felt in myself the density and weight of water teaming with life, every living being, every fish, crustacean, weed, and lily pad a part of me. The boy in the boat rowing over my surface was a part of me, too. I felt the forests of cedars around my perimeter, their roots reaching into the damp soil that was also an extension of me. I felt the currents running through me, invisible but tangible, exciting to me, thrilling. I felt the presence of water fowl bobbing on my surface, diving below now and then to capture a minnow in their beaks. When frightened they rose from my surface and I felt them shove away, then lift, the rhythmic draft of their wings wafting gently over my skin. I felt the night air cooling and saw the mist forming at the coves, rising a few inches from my surface.

The dream took me back to the day when I was ten. We had moved from the suburbs of Detroit to a house on the lake sixty miles north of the city. A neighbor had given me an old wooden rowboat with a plank bottom and a pair of very worn oars that rattled in the locks when I rowed. The boat had leaked like a sieve, but I pulled it out of the water, turned it upside down, and, after letting it dry in the sun for nearly a week, tarred the bottom to seal the narrow cracks that had let in the water. That's the way it was done by everyone I knew who owned a similar boat. Every year I scraped off the previous year's coating, pressed linseed oil caulking into the cracks, then repainted the bottom with thick black tar.

I loved that boat, shabby though it was. Others noticed only its rotting boards and squeaking oarlocks, but to me that skiff was the fulfillment of my fondest dreams. The first year I owned it, I spent hours on the lake rowing. I loved rowing in the evening, particularly when the sun was just setting and there was no one else on the water. Ours was a secluded lake, with only a dozen or so families who lived there year-round, the rest summer residents who came from the suburbs from June to September to escape the heat. So in the fall and early spring there was solitude.

On the lake alone at night, I felt cradled among earth, water, and sky, and whenever I rowed the private horrors that haunted me on land became part of a world a universe away. On the lake alone at night, the boundaries of my body dissolved. I went deep, deep into the watery depths of infinite consciousness, deep into myself and beyond it, far beyond it. Rowing, I felt every muscle and bone of my body, felt every cell of me strain against the oars, and lost myself, completely, in the wonder of it.

Out on the lake alone at night, the mystery of it all opened to me, and I knew the reason for the dream of the boat. It was to show me, beyond all reasonable doubt, that the mystery was enough, that it would never make itself known to us so I should give up the effort. On the lake alone at night, it became clear, in the stars, in the space between the stars, and in the endless flowing of water, that it would always be enough just to bask in the mystery. Just bask in it . . . that was all I would ever want or need.

So, four decades later I still draw from that boyhood memory. There were lessons in those experiences with my beloved boat that went far beyond my understanding at the time. It has taken me a lifetime even to begin to appreciate the meaning—that we are all one, not only humans and all other life, but that which we do not ordinarily think of as being sensate, like water and rocks and sky. There is something unknown, something as essential as water, that runs through all of us, the mystery that makes it possible not only to experience each other but to be each other.

Many years after I had left home, and many years after that boat of my dreams had rotted into oblivion, I came upon the idea of peak experiences in a book by Abraham Maslow. In it he spoke of how, during moments of the peak experience in our lives, we have the feeling of merging with our surroundings, of being "at one" with the universe. At the same time, we may also be most idiosyncratically ourselves. So, in peak experiences, we apparently confront our most essential selves as we come face to face with a power much greater than ourselves.

Out of the peak experiences of my life, particularly the kinds of epiphanies I relate here, there has come, time and time again, imagery and knowledge that I draw upon constantly as a writer. I look upon the memories of such moments as the creative wellsprings for my profession and from which I have drawn much strength in my life in general.

When my father was dying nearly twenty years ago, those early experiences on the lake, I believe, formed a guiding dream that would serve not only my father and me but the rest of my family as well. The story is worth telling, if only for the rich imagery that guided me through those difficult days of his passing.

I had not been in close communication with my parents for several years when I received a call from my brother saying that Dad was in the hospital and was very ill. At seventy-nine, he was not expected to survive the cancer that was invading his body. Shocked by this news I retreated to my study, and after meditating for several minutes recalled a dream I'd recorded in a journal three months earlier. I went to the journal, opened it to the page in question, and read the following:

> I am on a dock at the edge of a lake, a very big lake where I cannot see the other shore. It may be an ocean or perhaps it is a sea which has infinite borders, stretching on forever. It is dusk. I have led my father down a long ramp to a pier, where

a boat is waiting. My father is nervous, reluctant to do what he is about to do, but he has screwed up his courage and is doing it anyway. The boat I lead him to is a wooden speedboat but not of any make or design I've ever seen before. The man who owns it is standing on the pier waiting. As we approach, he greets my father and they shake hands. There is an immediate camaraderie established. The boatman expresses a kind of melancholy that I cannot quite identify. He seemed aware that this was going to be a difficult trip for my father, that there was a sadness about whatever it was they were embarking on. My father and the boatman turn their attention to the front deck of the boat, which is a beautifully finished mahogany. Since my father is a cabinet maker, he has a deep appreciation for such work. He and the boatman talk about the wood, how it was finished, etc. The boatman seems very proud and the two of them really get into this exchange of information. Finally the boatman says something to my father and my father turns to me and says it is time for him to go. We hug and kiss goodbye. My father and the other man get into the boat. I help them shove off, and in moments they are moving out over the water toward the East and toward the endless horizon. I stand on the pier watching until I can no longer see them, and I know that I will never see my father again.

When I read the dream, I again recalled the years on the lake when I was a child. The dream clearly reconnected me with that period. But there was also a message I had not recognized the night I'd recorded the dream. Not knowing that my father was ill at the time I had not thought that the image of the strange boat and boatman could also be an archetype, the boatman who comes to carry the dying person to the other side. Now, knowing that my father was dying, the meaning of the dream struck me to the core. For several minutes I felt shocked by the poignancy of the vision. And in the next moment I realized that the imagery was rich with other meaning. I was to be the one to lead my father to the dock and to the waiting boat.

This dream and happier memories of my early life on the lake mingled together in my mind. For one thing, I took the dream as a message that I was to be with my father and in some way that I had yet to discover assist him in his passage. I immediately made airline reservations and the next evening was with him and my family. I saw him in the hospital, very ill and fully conscious for all too fleeting episodes.

In the weeks that ensued, I spent many hours, as did my mother and brothers, sitting at Dad's bedside. I found that when I sat with him and meditated on the dream, I first saw only an empty dock. Then, the boat began to appear, first on the distant horizon, then clearer and clearer, until one day it was tied to the pier, the boatman beside it, waiting. For two days I saw my father and me going down the ramp to the pier, then meeting the boatman, just as I'd seen it in my dream. On the third day, exhausted and in need of deep rest, I went with my brother to my parents' home. At 3:10 a.m. the hospital called. Dad had passed over silently and effortlessly in his sleep.

The rich imagery of my original peak experience has guided me not only at those moments of great challenge, such as my father's death, but also in shaping and discovering ideas about my relationship to my world, to my craft, and to myself and my loved ones. Clearly there's a poetry about peak experiences

that transports us beyond ourselves, that gives us access to images and knowledge that perhaps goes far beyond everyday understanding. At such moments we are truly launched into the
eye of the mystery, where seemingly unlimited resources open
to us. We are never more ourselves than we are at such moments, never larger, yet we also confront the smallness of our
individual lives. As often as not, peak experiences liberate me
from virtually all fear; basking in the mystery, the recognition
of the truth that I will one day die, that I will give up this physical existence, no longer scares me. At least not for now.

As I trace back the image of me on the lake, I cannot find
where it begins because it stretches far back through my consciousness, perhaps emanating from the Norwegian seafaring
genes that came through my grandfather. From as far back as I
can remember, I have felt the pull of the sea, longed as a child
of six or seven to sit in my own boat on the waves. I must have
been eight or nine when I made a boat, crudely hammering together some boards and making a trailer for my bike to haul it
to a narrow creek a half-mile from home before we moved to
the lake. I still recall that long, anxious trip through the streets
with the boat slipping off the trailer several times. (It was a
terrible disappointment, as it turned out. The boat sank to the
bottom of the creek the instant I slipped it into the water. I
came home with a tin can full of crawfish that I kept alive in a
fish tank for nearly a week.)

What becomes clear to me is that our peak experiences are
dictated as much from within as from without. Ancient imagery, maybe stretching back for many generations, guided me
to the water and to the source of my first boat. The physical
experience of rowing on the lake revivified images and sensa-
tions that were not of my making, I am convinced of that. And

so not only are our peak experiences the wellsprings of our creative lives, but they connect us with the collective consciousness that has no boundaries or limits.

Even Ocean, the Titan Lord of the great river that encircled the earth, as the ancients told the myth, began much further back in time. And Nereus, Old Man of the Sea, who Hesiod described as completely trustworthy, always revealing the truth, and whose daughters, the Naids, danced even in the fountains and springs of Mother Earth, spoke to us humans from a place more ancient.

I think of my dream of the boatman. The Roman poet Virgil, describing the geography of the underworld, told of the path to Acheron, the river of woe, merging with Cocytus, the river of lamentation, both included on the journey of our souls out of this life and into the next. He told of Charon, the aging boatman who ferried souls of the dead over the water to the farther bank where they were judged and either condemned to eternal torment or blessed and sent to the blissful Elysian Fields. Water runs through our veins, extending far, far back; I have an idea that what we draw upon today is timeless, stretching not only around the earth but as far back as the Word itself, from which God made the world.

If all this is true, and I believe it is, then our peak experiences connect us with the original creative force. In a hundred lifetimes of the most prolific literary outpouring we could never exhaust this limitless supply. How odd it seems that such a universal and timeless source could also connect us so unequivocally with our most individualistic identities!

9: Higher Creativity and the Essential Wound

Well, mythology tells us that where you stumble, there your treasure is. . . . The world is a match for us and we're a match for the world. And where it seems most challenging lies the greatest invitation to find deeper and greater powers in ourselves.

JOSEPH CAMPBELL

I don't believe you have to suffer to be a good writer. But I suspect that if you come through life unscathed you also come through without much of a story to tell. Consider all the effort and self-control it would require to completely escape all pain and travail. Caution like that would be a full-time job, leaving little opportunity, or maybe even energy, for the demands of just plain living, much less writing. Fortunately, few of us have to worry much. Besides, it's been my experience that writers in particular aren't richly endowed with the good-sense gene that keeps more sober types out of trouble.

As for how much trouble is necessary, I can't really say. But I think that too much angst saps our creative juices and too little turns them rancid. Most writers I know do their best when the hard times are safely behind them. In this respect, it's probably safe to say that creative muses earn their salt by providing the power of reflection and 20/20 hindsight. Without that, we'd have to look elsewhere for the detachment required to work with the really tough material.

There is tremendous energy around our personal travails and woes, and we'd be fools not to tap its creative potential. When I think about the literature that's really moved me, it's often been written by people who dared to look into the shadows where most of us manage to shove the stuff that's too shameful or scary. I think about something Franz Kafka said: "There are many possibilities before me, but under which rock do they lie?" A friend of mine who writes poetry told me that quote, then added, "You know, I always picture being out for a walk in the woods when I come upon this damp, glistening rock, lift it up, turn it over, and there reaching out to me, clamoring to escape the light, are a million squirming centipedes, a whole world of spiny legs protruding from these dark writhing bodies."

I believe all writers write in an effort to heal something in their lives, though I suspect that's why most people do whatever it is they do. Writers and other people in the arts are just a little more obvious about it. A lot of what we have to learn in this craft is what we say about our wounds. When I was a teenager I poured over the novels of William Faulkner, and I have little doubt that I am still guided—perhaps hypnotized—by what I learned from him. When he talked about his writing he insisted that to be really good writers we must draw creative inspiration from our life experiences, which will give depth to whatever we have to say. And above all, he knew that it was from our wounds that we often learned the most valuable lessons, the ones we could pass on to others through our writing.

In December 1950 Faulkner was awarded the Nobel Prize for Literature. For years I had a tape recording of the acceptance speech he gave, which I listened to whenever I needed some encouragement with my writing. In that address he described what he thought were the responsibilities of the writer in modern life:

> He (the writer) must teach himself that the basest of all things is to be afraid; and teaching himself that, forget it forever, leaving no room in his workshop for anything but the old verities and truths of the heart, the old universal truths lacking which any story is ephemeral and doomed—love and honor and pity and pride and compassion and sacrifice.

Ruminating on those words, I asked myself what it was about fear that made it worthy of the writer's efforts. And his speech also suggested to me that there was something to be gained by taking what we have discovered in the best and worst moments of our lives and somehow making them universal so that they might have meaning for other people.

Our greatest fears, I believe, don't come from the fear of physical threat or even death, but from something deeper. Fear grows out of the dread of not being able to trust our perceptions about the way the world works. My mother was fond of telling a story that had happened when I was about four-and-a-half years old. A playmate and I had watched our cat giving birth to four kittens. It was a frightening but magical moment for both of us. Afterward, we sat on the back porch of my parents' house and talked about what had happened. According to my mother, my friend said, "Humans get born the same way, you know. They come out of the mother's body." I stood up and, with my hands placed stubbornly on my hips, said, "They do not! They come from the hospital!"

Although my mother always told this as a "cute story" about my growing up, I think I always recognized that something more important had happened to me that day. The four-year-old had created a reality in his mind based on humans coming from hospitals. I had put together a limited picture of the world—at least where birth was concerned—based on the scant information that would have filtered down to me at that age. I probably also had a certain amount of denial because it was just too preposterous to think that humans would really have to go through the pain and indignity of all that spilt blood and bodily fluids.

However you look at it, my discovery of the real birth process shattered a model of life that I'd held in my mind. And that shattering is always both a wound and a terrible awakening. We're reminded at such times that what we believe isn't always what really is, and we'd be fools to claim there's not a certain panic, particularly if we don't at least entertain the possibility that there's a power greater than ourselves. Life is filled with such moments, of course, with the truth constantly poking fun at our efforts to understand our lives. As the saying goes, "If you really want to make God laugh, tell her your plans."

We make sense of the world through creating inner pictures of what our lives are about. Usually these pictures more or less work, so we're somewhat justified in believing in them, in depending on them. Then something happens that pushes the limits, that reminds us we have fabricated these pictures out of our limited view of what makes the universe tick.

What's more, we can't always depend on other people—even our loved ones—to comfort or protect us, or even to see our needs, when the pictures fail us.

These essential wounds are at the core of our humanness. They occur when we confront the outer limits of our abilities, that is, the limits of that inner vision we've constructed of the world from the vast accumulation of our life experiences. We find at such times that life itself is always greater, more expansive, richer and at the same time simpler and more complex than anything we can ever hold in our minds. To tell the story of the moments when we've suffered and then healed our essential wounds is to reveal a universal insight that extends far beyond the particulars.

It's difficult to pick out one example of an essential wound from the stories from my writing classes, but I think of Barry, a man in his early forties who came to me after I'd assigned the class to write a short piece about essential wounds. Barry said there was something he wanted to write, but he could not guarantee that he would be able to finish it, and if I wanted him to read it to the class he was afraid he might not be able to do that, either.

Thinking he was overdramatizing, I told him to do his best and assured him that I would not force him to read his piece to the class. He did not want to tell me what his wound was, but he thought he would tell me the next day, whether he read or not.

I was surprised in class the following day because Barry was the first to announce that he would like to read his story. His voice trembled as he prefaced his story with a description of his father, who, he said, figured into his story in a way Barry had never been quite able to fit.

"My dad," he said, "was in the Korean war, and when he came back he was without his right leg. He would never talk about what happened and whenever anyone in the family brought it up, he became very agitated, told everyone to shut up and often vacated the room. The only thing he ever said about the war was that it was in the past and there was nothing to be gained by talking about it. He went on to become a very successful businessman and, I suppose, a good father."

With this preface, Barry read what he'd written. He kept his head bowed as he read, never looking up and never making eye contact with anyone in the room. The piece started out when he was a freshman at a college in the Midwest. It was a beautiful, sunny day, and he was walking across campus with some friends. There had been antiwar demonstrations for the past couple of days, and there was another rally going on that afternoon. Suddenly, he thought he heard a car backfire, but the sounds came from the center of campus, where there were no streets. Several more reports rang out, and then he realized he was hearing gunshots.

For some reason he raced toward the sound, rather than away from it. As he came around the corner of one of the buildings, he saw the crowd gathered on the lawn. There were soldiers from the National Guard standing a few yards away with their guns drawn. He remembered thinking that they looked like pretend soldiers, young men like himself dressed up in uniforms and carrying weapons.

Someone he barely knew grabbed him by the arm and pulled him through the crowd, jabbering away that Barry's friend had been shot. And then he remembered dropping to one knee by the limp body of the young man who'd been his friend, a new friend, and a young woman in her teens scream-ing at the soldiers and holding the young man's head in her lap. The place was Kent State where four students died and nine were wounded by guardsmen that day.

As Barry read his piece, he broke down and wept several times. But each time he rallied his courage and went on.

> After the ambulances came and went, I found myself back at the campus center. I remember there were huge lines at the telephone booths, where weeping students were calling their families at home to tell them what had happened and to as-sure them they were okay. Reporters from the newspapers were already milling around, as were the television cameras. I waited in line for nearly an hour, trying to believe and not believe what was happening. I needed to talk to someone, to try and tell them what was going on with me and maybe get plugged back into a reality I could trust again. When it came my turn to use the phone, I called my dad at his work. He had always been my source of strength when I was a kid. I re-ally looked up to him.
>
> "He's in a meeting," his secretary told me.
>
> "It's important," I told her. "You'll have to interrupt him."
>
> I waited for about five long minutes, and finally my dad got on the line.
>
> "Something terrible has happened," I told him. "I had to talk to you."
>
> He asked me to make it brief because he was in an impor-tant meeting. I described what had happened. There was only silence on the line for a long time. I said, "Dad, did you hear me?"

"Yes, I heard you," he replied, his voice cold, more detached and distant than I ever remembered him being. And then, "You're okay? You're safe?"

"I think so," I told him. "I wasn't shot or anything."

"Good," he said. Then, "I have to get back to my meeting."

And that was it! I stood there in the cramped phone booth, holding the dead receiver in my hand and feeling empty and confused.

The horror of the Kent State killings was a big enough wound to last anyone a lifetime. There wasn't a person in the class who would have questioned that. After all, how could any of us create an inner vision of a world where the innocents could be shot down in cold blood? But Barry wasn't finished with his story. He went on to describe how the memory of that day replayed over and over in his dreams, year after year. He never felt safe after that, though he'd learn to walk down a street with his fear and not cave in every time he heard a car backfire or a sudden sound that he couldn't identify.

"The real wound for me," he continued, "wasn't in what the soldiers did that day. I've been over that a million times in my mind. There were crisis counselors to help us after it happened, and I've spent years in therapy. But talking about the soldiers and the killing doesn't help anymore. In fact it never did. Every time I think about it, I remind myself that there are thousands of people in the world who see things like that happen every day, and they live with it. Why can't I?"

Andrea, a woman in her late seventies, was attending the workshop that day. She'd been very reserved through the previous four sessions, and I'd begun to wonder if she was getting anything at all from the class. So I was surprised when she was the first to speak up.

"Barry," she said. "Your essential wound was that your father dropped the ball. You know what I mean, don't you?"

Barry stared across the room at her, and his eyes filled with tears. He could only nod.

"I've never witnessed anything that horrifying," Andrea continued. "But your courage to tell us that story has been very healing for me. We're always dropping the ball, all of us, or we're having it dropped on us. We want so much to believe that we will support each other in times of crisis—but the truth is we often don't. It's not that we don't care or that we're withholding. It's that we can't. Something has happened in our own past that we don't dare look at. We don't know how. We're too busy pushing back our own grief and terror."

She said that Barry's story about his father's wound re-minded her that our weaknesses and faults as human beings often have a long history over which we have little control. She said, "Your father couldn't quite break free of his own his-tory and what he didn't want to talk about. To give you what you needed that day, he would have had to face his own fear and grief and maybe his shame, and he could not do that. But you broke the chain and escaped from your history and his when you had the courage to tell us this story." She paused, seemed to be thinking about what she'd just said, then added, "Your telling this story has helped me to heal. I want you to know that. You didn't drop the ball, and I want to thank you for that."

I'm not sure I understood everything that happened in the workshop that day. But it has become a model for me of why we write, of why we bother with the often painful task of putting our stories on paper. Each time I think about Barry's story, I'm reminded once again that the story, poem, or book we write isn't the real end product. Our writing isn't finished until it's read. In that respect, Andrea was the quintessential reader that day, revealing that sometimes, when we can summon the guts to begin telling our truth, the effect ripples into other people's lives in ways that are as unpredictable as they are courageous. And it becomes part of an evolving consciousness that maybe someday will allow all of us to embrace all of life, to no longer block out what is painful or distasteful. Stories like this are proof that we truly do build bridges between our own consciousness and others' at those moments. Certainly there was a powerful bridge built that day between Barry and Andrea, and perhaps others in the class.

Although all of us experience numerous essential wounds throughout our lives, usually one or two are pivotal. Earlier in this book I mentioned a motorcycle accident I had that became a turning point for me. So much came out of that near-fatal event that I have to look upon it with gratitude rather than with regret or bitterness. When I look back, it seems to me that my life before the accident had been chaotic and murky, driven by a strange combination of naivete, arrogance, and downright confusion. After it was a clarity I'd never known. It is worth telling here.

At the time of the accident, I had recently completed my college education, my son was almost two years of age, and my writing was beginning to be published. Yet, my life was crumbling around me. Earlier in the year, my wife and I had made the decision to divorce. We hadn't filed papers, but it was clear to us that we would soon. We were still in that painfully befuddling place that every divorcee knows only too well—when every moment we are apart convinces us our divorce would be the worst mistake we'd ever make, and every moment together convinces us that we can't end the bond soon enough.

That day my wife and I had made a date to meet at the park near where she and my son were living. Somehow, we crossed signals and she didn't come. I was furious with her, disappointed that I would not see my son and certain she had deliberately not shown up just to punish me (it turned out I was the one who'd mixed up the date).

After waiting more than an hour, I jumped on my motorcycle and took off, determined to go to a lawyer immediately and get the whole nightmare over with. It was a gray, overcast day in San Francisco, and the traffic was light as I approached a stoplight. I was driving along at fifteen or twenty miles an hour when a heaving old Pontiac careened around the corner, the driver swerving to my side of the road. I glanced to the left, looking for an escape route, saw the space I needed but hesitated, angry, stubbornly willing the car out of my path. The next moment I was in the air, flying over the hood of the car. Then I was lying on my back in the street. I did not make an effort to get up. The only sensation I could identify was pain and there was no doubt that I was badly injured.

Two years earlier I'd learned to meditate. As I lay in the street wracked in pain, I began counting my breaths and focusing on a Zen koan I'd been taught. And in the process I calmed myself enough to assess my injuries.

Moments later the ambulance arrived and after a brief but agonizing ride to the emergency room I found myself surrounded by the doctors and nurses as they worked over me.

For the next couple of hours I was probed, prodded, x-rayed, and catherized. Tubes were pushed up my nose, an IV installed, and a screw was bored through my shin bone with what looked exactly like a carpenter's hand drive. After that, a traction weight was strung from a rack over my bed, attached by a series of ropes and pulleys to the shiny bolt in my shin bone, and I was wheeled into a ward housing thirty-five men waiting for their broken bones to heal.

At last it was quiet. A doctor and nurse came to my bedside, asked me some questions, wrote some notes on a clipboard, then gave me a shot of something that burned like fire in my right buttock. I remember asking how long I'd have to stay in the hospital with my leg attached to the bed. The doctor shrugged. "Six weeks or so if everything goes okay," he said.

Before I could recover from the shock of the doctor's announcement he had turned away and was gone. I felt thoroughly abandoned, confused, and angry. I wanted to scream out to them—to someone, anyone!—to have one human being calmly tell me, in plain language, what was going on. Then, within minutes, I really didn't care anymore. The shot was taking effect. I felt warm and safe, secure and loved. I imagined that the vast ward of groaning injured men were all my friends and I was a kid away at summer camp, looking forward to a long, blissful vacation. At last I slipped off to sleep.

Six weeks is a long time to be flat on one's back, totally dependent on others for one's most basic needs, with little capacity for anything but reading, talking to people in the neighboring beds, brooding over one's fate, or thinking. I had visits from friends, which helped break up the day. One was my wife (who later became perhaps my most important link with the outside world). Two days after the accident, she opened the drawer of my bedside table and noticed my wristwatch. She looked at the shattered crystal and noted the time the mangled hands were trying to indicate.

"Did this stop when you were hit?"

"Yes," I said. The crystal was pressed against the hands, and a large dent in the case indicated quite clearly that it would never run again.

"It says 4:20," she said. "I have to tell you something. We were across the bay in Berkeley about that time, at Quentin's birthday party. Nathan [our son] was playing, and then he suddenly stopped and went over to the chair where I was sitting and wanted to be held. He became very depressed, and when I asked him what was wrong he said, 'Man crashed. Man hurt!' He repeated it several times."

She couldn't make sense of it yet, not knowing about the accident. About a half-hour later Nathan still felt bad, so they left the party early, getting home at about six o'clock.

Had it been a mere coincidence that Nathan talked about the man getting hurt at about the same time that I was hit? I didn't know how to answer that, but I did know that the bond between my son and me had always been unusually strong. I was deeply moved by the possibility that our link might be such that he would have sensed my trouble from thirty miles away. What pained me almost as much as my broken bones was the realization that if this mystical bond with my son was real, it meant he might literally have to share my suffering.

After his mother left I spent a lot of time thinking about that connection. I remembered hearing about such things, but I had never had this kind of apparent confirmation. I'd read Jung in college and remembered his work on synchronicity, or what he called "acausal relationships" between life events.

Jung told the story of waking up in the middle of the night feeling that someone had entered his hotel room. He turned on a light just to make certain no one was there. There wasn't, of course, and the door was securely locked. When he returned to bed, he felt a pain in the back of his mouth and the back of his head, neither of which were familiar complaints to him.

Because of the strange occurrence, he noted the time in a journal at his bedside. At breakfast he was handed a telegram. A patient of his, living in a city a considerable distance away, had committed suicide during the night by putting a gun in his mouth and pulling the trigger. He had died within minutes of the time Dr. Jung had awakened and experienced the pain.

If one really could sense another's distress across the miles, it means there perhaps is a mystical connection among loved ones that transcends the boundaries of time and space. A prisoner of my bed, I had a lot of time to contemplate such things, and from that vantage point I became more and more intent on asking some essential questions.

I noticed, for example, that all the distress I had been feeling about my impending divorce had almost magically dissolved. I recognized that the final separation was inevitable and saw myself carrying through everything that must be done to complete it. The terrible angst I'd felt about the breakup and, in particular, the separation from my young son, seemed to lift. The sobering experience of having one's life threatened, as mine had been, caused me to see my emotions in a new light.

Strangely enough, this wound was an awakening. For the first time that I could recall I was able to stand outside myself for long periods, to fully participate in my life but at the same time have a new detachment, a consciousness about what I was doing. In a dream one night I sharply focused in on what my distress about the divorce was about. I had loved my son's mother passionately. She had seemed to be the fulfillment of a vision that was deeply ingrained in my very being, my perception of perfect love, and I had thoroughly believed that we would be together forever. But in spite of help from therapists and our desire to make our marriage work, it didn't. For the year or two before our final separation, I'd asked over and over, "What had gone wrong? How could it possibly be that our relationship had gotten so far off track?"

There were answers, of course. There always are. But were they meaningful answers? And what did it matter if they were? It was clear that our marriage was over. I grieved for the destruction of my vision, but more than that I grieved for what I feared the most—my separation from my son. How would it affect him?

In a dream, however, a clear voice told me that all I had to do was let go of my old perceptions and I'd discover an entirely new vision of love. But fear stopped me, though what I feared the most was that I would never be able to trust my passions again. That would always be my struggle—the danger that I would never again act on anything I felt passionately about. I would be hyper-vigilant, always trying to protect myself from further hurt. My fear was like a rigid sentry guarding the old vision, telling me it was too precious to abandon. The alternative to my fear was to follow my passions, recognizing the risk and doing it anyway. But first I had to empty myself, to let go of the vision I had cherished. It was hard. It was as if I'd been given a puzzle to solve, with all the pieces neatly laid out for me and crystal clear, but with the solution to the puzzle constantly eluding me. And strangely enough there was something remarkably familiar about the whole thing; all of it an old theme that I'd never been able to get fully in focus.

Clarity about what I must do to embrace my passion was one of many gifts that came out of my wound. Another had to do with a sense of separation I'd always felt. Since early childhood I'd always had the impression that my life was a mistake, that I'd somehow been delivered to the wrong parents at a wrong time in history or on the wrong planet. I'd always had this sense of being "special," not necessarily in a wonderful way, the way a parent says a child is special, but special in a sense that made it virtually impossible for me to feel a connection with other people. In the hospital my specialness was exaggerated because here I was, a nice middle-class young man, with a college education and really nice parents living in the Midwest, tied to a bed in a public hospital, surrounded by men who I normally would never meet.

In the bed on my right was Percy, a man in his fifties who'd broken half the bones in his body when he fell through a skylight. "I was drunk," he told me. Across the way was Reggie, a black kid about eighteen who'd been shot in the leg. The gunman had been a shopkeeper on Fillmore Street who caught Reggie breaking in through a rear window. Reggie's femur had been badly shattered but he was just counting his blessings that he was still alive. The shopkeeper had intended to kill him. He had his left wrist handcuffed to the bed because he was under arrest. The cop who guarded him during the day was a young rookie who was pretty nice to him and most of the time treated him like a friend.

About half the ward was black. And from the conversations that went around I figured that for many of the people there the hospital care they were getting was a lot better than they were otherwise accustomed to.

One afternoon, a wiry black man about fifty walked over to me and started talking. His name was Jimmy Gray. I remembered his name because I had a friend in high school by the same name. He asked what had happened to me, and I told him. Because he was ambulatory, he didn't look like he had anything wrong with him. He answered my question: "They're going to fix my hernia." He admitted he was scared. He'd never had an operation. He explained that because he was a heroin addict they couldn't "put me out," so he was going to have the operation with only a local anesthetic.

He told me his story in an easy, matter-of-fact manner I might use to tell a friend I liked coffee. He asked if I liked the blues. I said I did, and we talked about blues singers we enjoyed. We both liked Mississippi Fred McDowell, Muddy Waters, Lightning Hopkins, and the Chicago blues singers like Jimmy Rush and Joe Williams. He had known a lot of musicians, most of them from New Orleans, people I'd never heard of, and he'd written lyrics for some. He asked if I'd like to hear something he wrote. I said sure. He stood beside my bed, looking out the window, talking his blues like a long poem. The words told about hard times and good times, about falling in love and broken hearts. Sometimes Jesus' name came up. They told about struggling to stay alive when there was nothing to live for, about friendships that went wrong or that endured the worst kinds of trials. They told about dreams for a better life with a sense of hope that defied all reason, given what his life had become.

When he was done he turned to me and asked how I liked it. I couldn't answer because I was crying. I'm not sure if the tears were because I'd been moved by his lyrics or because they made me feel sorry for myself. He just looked at me and said, "I understand," then patted my shoulder like a caring mother, turned away, and walked out of the room. I never saw him again, though one of the orderlies told me the operation had been successful. He was released, back to the streets, a few days later.

I thought a lot about Jimmy Gray, about the lyrics he'd written, and I even entertained the idea of writing the words on paper for him. (He'd told me he couldn't read or write.) But mostly, a passage from the Bible kept coming back to me: "Mankind is one." Those were words I'd puzzled over for a long time. They'd never made sense to me. But that day they did. Because Jimmy Gray's lyrics revealed to me that in spite of the gaps created by our ethnic backgrounds, and in spite of the fact that I had a college education and he couldn't write, and in spite of the vast chasm between our socioeconomic statuses, we had a great deal in common. We both suffered the same heartaches and celebrated the same joys. We both reached out for hope. Somewhere behind the obvious masks of our differences we were one.

In the weeks following, the old sense of loneliness, of specialness, of not belonging, dissolved. For the first time I felt that I belonged, that there was a basic truth in the biblical passage—Mankind is one—that could not be denied. It was a liberation for me, a casting off of a self-imposed shell that insulated me from the world. Instead of wanting to keep my distance from the other men in the ward, I felt a desire to somehow serve them. During the next weeks I sometimes read aloud to the man in the next bed, who could not read though he got letters every week from his daughter. Other men in the ward asked me to write notes for them when for one reason or another they couldn't do it themselves.

I felt good serving others, even in small ways. It is all too easy to feel both helpless and useless when one is bedridden, and these little tasks helped to keep me sane. But much more, experiencing myself as joined with the others ultimately opened a doorway to a kind of love I had never known, though it would take me several years to really begin to understand.

The accident that day, and the events leading up to it, literally tore me out of the life I'd known and offered me the gift of a new perspective, far broader and richer than anything I'd ever imagined. It showed me that perhaps I had a choice about how to live. I could, in effect, let go of my old way of looking at the world by knowing there were other options, and to begin creating a life for myself instead of having it just happen to me. Certainly I didn't have all the pieces—far from it! But without a doubt what I learned from this wound became a great creative source, showing me that life could be approached far more creatively than I'd been taught was possible.

I am convinced that every essential wound, by its nature, has the potential for opening each of us to the full potential of our soul. It's not a matter of the universe providing us with the challenges we supposedly need for our spiritual growth. I tend to believe in the universe's "benign indifference," as Camus once put it, and that God is something like a courageous and loving parent who gives us all we can take in, then lets us go on to live our lives the best we know how. I think that must have been what Joseph Campbell was talking about, too, in the quote at the start of this chapter—that "the world is a match for us and we're a match for the world. And where it seems most challenging lies the greatest invitation to find deeper and greater powers in ourselves."

It is our perceptions of the world, the inner vision of what we think life is about, that is challenged in every essential wound. Our true creativity comes when we start trying to sort out our perceptions, asking what the wound mirrors back to us, what it tells us about ourselves, what we need to let go of and what we need to learn to embrace. Then we take ourselves out of the role of victim. We see there's an alternative to the way we ordinarily look upon our grievances—that we can mine even our worst errors for the treasures they contain. When we look at our wounds this way, we invariably discover turning points, breakthroughs that carry us beyond the limits of everyday thinking. And like Barry, we can tell the stories that are truly important to tell, that reveal the hidden truths of our lives and the lives of others, thus building spiritual bridges between our consciousnesses and theirs.

Where do we begin? How do we start uncovering the treasures in our wounds? By simply mustering the courage to look at our lives unflinchingly. After that, the answers always come in a rush, fueling the creative fires without which a writer is little more than a typist with an attitude.

I can think of no better way to end this, the longest chapter in the book, than with the following quote from *Here All Dwell Free,* by Gertrud Mueller Nelson:

> Our responsibility, then, is to find and know the story that is our own. We then reach out to grapple with it, choosing to suffer the conflicts that pull us back into our fate and forward to our true selves. As we become healed and autonomous, we reenter our community and our history, offering

our gifts to benefit all and taking our place as cocreators of our personal and communal destinies. All three of these tasks, though developmental in nature, are not necessarily done in stair-step order, but cycle around and around, deeper and deeper, as we grow in consciousness and responsibility . . . only where we allow ourselves to be fully human can God meet us, and here we encounter our true selves, as if for the first time. Here all dwell free.

10: Higher Creativity and the Mask Self

Where is the I, the entity that decides what to do with the psychic energy generated by the nervous system? Where does the captain of the ship, the master of the soul, reside?

MIHALY CSIKSZENTMIHALYI

I have a friend who's a Catholic priest. Father Sean is a native of Ireland, speaks with a rich Irish brogue, laughs easily, and writes wonderful, thought-provoking sermons that sometimes would make the Pope squirm. A year ago he got his doctorate degree in psychology and has been preparing to take the state boards for his license as a psychotherapist. Last Christmas he conducted mass at a small church in the suburbs. His sermon was about remembering our true spiritual nature. He began by telling about a trip he'd recently taken to Disneyland. He went on all the rides, then became fascinated with Mickey Mouse, who wanders around the park talking to children.

Everywhere Father Sean looked, there was Mickey Mouse shaking hands with people, talking with children, keeping everyone's spirits up. And Father Sean began asking himself, "I wonder who that person is under the costume? What are they like at the end of the day, when they take off the Mickey Mouse suit?" Having shed the comic book character, how does that person treat members of their family, their wife, their kids, the neighbors?

For Father Sean, Mickey Mouse became a metaphor for the way we humans live. Like the person inside the Mickey Mouse suit, we assume a certain character, but soon forget that this "costume" is not our true self. This is not to say that we are like actors, deliberately choosing a certain character to play. On the contrary, we adopt and build that character ourselves, gradually and over a long time. Mostly, it happens so gradually that we barely notice what we're doing. By the time we're in high school, we're so deeply identified with the character that we assume this is who we are.

I have a friend in New Mexico who tells a wonderful story that illustrates how these costumes, these Mickey Mouse suits we wear, ultimately become so real to us that we fool even ourselves. When she was in her late twenties, my friend, a single mother, taught on a Zuni Indian reservation. It turned out to be a nearly ideal place to raise her child. The small-town atmosphere and generally loving community provided a quiet, protective environment. Her blond and blue-eyed daughter always stood out in stark contrast to her dark-skinned, brown-eyed playmates, but she got along well with the other children and was loved by everyone in the community.

One year, when the child was eight years old, she was sitting on a wall in Zuni watching kachina dances with her friend, a native American girl her same age. These dances are performed by men dressed in elaborate traditional costumes, each representing a spirit or force that exists in the Zuni religion. As the kachinas filed by, the bones and bells attached to

their costumes magically jingling and rattling with each dancing step, the Zuni girl turned to her blond-haired Anglo friend
and said, "Do you know the secret of the kachinas?" En-
tranced by the dancers, her friend shook her head. "No. What
is it?" The Zuni girl leaned close and whispered, "There's really people in there!"

Like the children watching the kachina dances, it's easy to
become so mesmerized by the costumes we wear that we finally believe they are the *real thing*. And to rediscover that
there is something more the costume is covering comes as a
kind of revelation. It's hard to remember that we came into
life without our Mickey Mouse suits on, that we in fact came
in as spiritual beings. Father Sean's point was that our life
spirit slips into its physical body, taking up residence in that
form in much the same way that a person playing Mickey
Mouse slips into a costume upon arriving for work at Disneyland every morning.

The Mickey Mouse metaphor is very close to what I call
the *mask self*. But for me the mask self is not a ready-made
character that we arbitrarily assume. Rather, it is something
we ourselves mold and create, though we do so on a more or
less unconscious level. In effect, the mask self is the product
of our own life experiences, the lessons we've learned along
the way through our essential wounds and our peak experiences. The mask self is the self we have constructed to feel
safe in the world. In many ways it functions as a shield, protecting our vulnerable inner self from the *slings and arrows* of
the outer world.

Years ago, I spent a lot of time with avant-garde theater
groups in San Francisco who were experimenting with using
masks in performance. I became fascinated by what happens

to both actor and audience when a person dons a mask. It is as if the mask takes over, becomes dominant over the actor. The best masks depict a certain character even before the actor puts it on, and when it's in place it tends to dictate what the actor will say and how he or she will move, think, and respond to other actors.

As spectators we tend to forget the actor under the mask and respond instead to the mask. If you've seen a group of children watching a puppet show (the puppet being another kind of mask), you'll recognize how thoroughly convincing a mask can be. When my son was still very small, he had a collection of hand puppets he played with; when I put a puppet over my hand, disguised my voice, and talked to Nathan, he would carry on long conversations with the puppet, as if I weren't there. I noticed the same thing with other children when Nathan's friends came to play. When they spoke with the puppets, they also took on disguised voices, just as I did when I worked the puppets. To me this meant that at some level the children knowingly participated in the puppets' fantasy world, not unlike what we all do with the mask self. We instinctively know there is a truth beyond the mask, but we willingly participate in maintaining the illusion that the mask is all there is.

One theater group I worked with, the San Francisco Mime Troupe, performed in the tradition of commedia dellarte, a theater form popular throughout Europe during the Middle Ages. Usually, those performances were given in public places, like open air markets, or during festivals. The plays had set story lines within which the actors improvised their lines. Sometimes the story carried an underlying political message, everything from the age-old sport of lambasting royalty to advocating revolution.

The San Francisco group performed in parks during the late sixties and early seventies, when we had active civil rights demonstrations and the antiwar movement was growing. So most of the troupe's performances dealt with those themes, often in powerful ways.

In the initial phase of putting a production together, the troupe's actors worked long hours with their masks and costumes. Many actors made their own masks or worked closely with the costumer so that the mask eventually came to be a blending of the actor's personality and the character they were to play. Then, at that magic moment when they walked on stage, the actors I had known backstage were completely transformed. I no longer saw them as people I'd had dinner with an hour earlier. It was as if the mask focused in on one portion of their own character, allowing them to exaggerate that aspect, ultimately developing it as a full character. At times the transformation would be frightening—as when the person who was a saint offstage became the arch villain behind a long-nosed mask and flowing black cape. Having assumed the character of the mask, the actor drew from a dark, shadowy side of his or her being, bringing it forth in the context of the loosely drawn script.

The years I spent in the theater were quite wonderful, though looking back on it I realize it was not the theater itself that interested me so much as what it taught me about our human capacities and the world of illusion that is our daily lives. The recognition that actors could become not just one character but many suggested to me that perhaps behind the mask self we present to the world in our day-to-day lives are many subcharacters, all playing important roles in our lives. Unbeknownst to me at the time, each revelation about our masks was taking me closer to the truth Father Sean described in his sermon.

At about the same time I was working in the theater, I was also part of a study on the use of hallucinogenics in psychotherapy. One weekend a peyote shaman introduced a small group of us to this ancient herb and its use in spiritual ritual. After ingesting what looked like small cactus apples, with the foulest taste one could ever imagine, I began to shiver uncontrollably. When the shaking finally settled down, I suddenly became warm and comfortable, almost euphoric, and began having beautiful visions, little bursts of brilliant colors all in elaborate, geometric shapes similar to the geometry of snowflakes, but with much more color and with no two exactly alike. This shower of colorful shapes was the welcoming celebration for events that were soon to follow.

I immediately started having vivid waking dreams. I saw beautiful landscapes, houses, the interiors of rooms, and people. At one point I had to go to the bathroom and had to walk through darkened rooms to get there. Along the way I met several dream-people and stopped to have short conversations with each one. In the dream space provided by the peyote, these people seemed no different than people I might meet on the street. Although I knew they were dream-people, they always appeared quite autonomous, speaking back, laughing, listening, often in unexpected ways.

By the time I returned to the room and the rest of the group, I was beginning to feel that all the dream-people I'd met and spoken with seemed familiar to me. I asked the shaman if he knew about such characters. Did they appear in this way for everyone? And who were they?

"Are they people you know in real life?" the shaman asked.

"No. Definitely not. Yet, when we speak to each other, I feel the way I do when I am around close friends. We can talk as if we've shared a long history together."

"Then they are from your dream world," he said. "They are the people from your inner world."

"Like characters I have created in my dreams?"

"Not exactly," he said. "In my tradition (he was of native American descent), it is believed that we take part in two different worlds, the world of dream and the world we most often refer to as *reality*. But according to our way, only the dream world is real. The reality we call the physical world is the illusion. That's just the opposite of the way most people are taught in the schools today. Our task in this life is to learn from the inner world and to understand how these two worlds can help each other."

I was skeptical about what he had to say. I could accept the idea that at a deep psychological level we might create different characters to represent aspects of ourselves. But the idea that these characters might have lives of their own, separate from us, seemed preposterous.

After the session I thought a lot about what the shaman had told me. And in the half-dozen or so sessions we had after that, I began exploring the dream-people that appeared. The first was Alycia, a woman in her late forties or early fifties, rather tall and of medium build, with curly salt and pepper hair cropped close to her head and soft brown eyes that always looked a little worried or distressed. I first saw her as a generous nurturer, a person who was always looking for ways she could help others, a kind of saint. After I'd made contact with her, I was puzzled by how I felt toward her. Frankly, though she seemed generous, self-effacing, and sincerely helpful to others—including me—I didn't like her. I felt threatened by her. In her presence I became deflated, weak, and resentful. It took me years to discover what that was all about; her helpfulness was motivated not so much by truly helping others as it was by a driving need to prove that she was a good person.

I wrestled with Alycia for years, sometimes seeing myself doing exactly what she was doing—rescuing people in need to prove that I was good. At other times I'd find myself drawn to people who, like Alycia, had a need to be helpful, and those relationships always proved disastrous. Then, an odd thing began to happen. Alycia began to change. It was as if she had suddenly seen what was going on in her life and that some of the work I'd been doing in my life—wrestling with the two sides of the nurturer—were being reflected on her. Somewhere we both recognized that we could never find the self-respect and self-love we'd been seeking on the path we'd been following. I began to see that instead of turning to the outside world for support and self-affirmation there was an inner wisdom from which I could draw that, quite simply, made me feel very good about myself.

As I learned to draw from my place of inner wisdom, the need to prove I was good began to diminish. I often found myself lured into the helping role, but it was now in a different light. In my writing and teaching, for example, I began attracting readers and students who wanted to learn particular skills. They came for this reason, rather than to be rescued from themselves. And it was after that subtle but important shift occurred that I learned how teaching and learning can be the same thing—that as teachers we are doubly blessed because we learn at least as much from our students as they learn from us.

Today, whenever I think or dream of Alycia, it is love and admiration I feel for her. She and I have both changed, and it is impossible to determine which of us initiated these shifts in our perspectives. The distrust and ambivalence I had felt so strongly toward her is no longer there. It is nice to believe that we have come a long way together, and we recognize that we, too, have been teachers to each other.

Although I have many characters in my dream world, my relationship with Alycia is probably the best illustration of how we can work with the inner world. In writing a novel, getting in touch with our personal dream-people becomes a key source of our creativity. In nonfiction it is our struggles with the issues we have with our dream-people, or their counterparts in the external world, that provide us with our greatest passions. And it's these passions we need to keep us motivated through the long, tedious task of writing a book. When we're connected with these passions, issues such as disciplining ourselves to write fall by the wayside. Passion, after all, is its own motivator. Ultimately, the question no longer is how we can discipline ourselves to write, but how we can discipline ourselves to stop.

Behind the mask self we find a myriad of dream-people, perhaps a whole world of them, an entire planet! Just as in our waking lives, some will be more prominent than others. In an entire lifetime, it is impossible to get to them all. But I believe that it is through the synergy of the inner and outer worlds that we lift the mask, ultimately stripping it away enough to catch at least a fleeting glimpse of our souls, our true spiritual nature.

Part of the job of writing is to excite and entertain our readers; but the other part is to establish clearer relationships with the inner world. I don't think we can really accomplish the first part of this job description without accomplishing the second. Our creative passion comes through as we become fully engaged in this dance between inner and outer, and that passion is what makes our writing electric.

I don't think all writers consciously explore dreamtime, at least not the way I describe. But there's no doubt in my mind that, conscious or not, we all draw extensively from this source.

Remember that the mask self is that part of ourselves we dare present to the world. It is a way of being we have put together, frequently in a rather haphazard way and often through the trials and errors of our lives. For the most part, the mask self protects us from having to look more closely at the dream-people that lie behind it. It protects the more vulnerable creatures of our inner world.

In an ideal universe, there would be no need for the mask self, and no need to protect our inner worlds. We would simply come into life, into the arms of loving parents who would take one look at us and with complete and total awe exclaim, "My God, what a wonderful creature! I wonder what gifts she is bringing into this world? How can I ever discover what these are, nurture them, and allow her to fully blossom?" But as parents we're seldom that magnanimous, insightful, or secure in ourselves. Out of our fears and insecurities we press in on the infant. Rather than asking how we might nurture this new being so that she can deliver her new gifts to the world, we become overly responsible. We think, "Oh, I must groom and shape this little being into a responsible citizen. I must make certain that she is well disciplined, that she gets a good education so she can get a good-paying job or meet a rich husband." As well meaning as these motives may be, the gifts the child brings into the world may be completely ignored or shoved aside and that child, in effect, will become invisible.

Years ago I spent two weeks in a college course entitled "The Psychology of Education," in which the instructor said that as infants we come into the world like empty vessels and our task as parents and teachers is to fill those vessels. I sat through three hours of lectures before I walked out, convinced that this approach to education was inherently destructive. I didn't know what offended me so deeply then, but something did. To me there was an element of the instructor's philosophy that was painful and mean, and I found myself reacting out of proportion to what had been said. But maybe my outrage was justified after all.

I think what I got in touch with that day was a wound most of us suffer when we're growing up—that somehow, in the course of even the most loving parents' efforts to *bring us up,* who we really are is ignored. We get wiped out, or nearly so. In our early years we recognize how dependent we are on the adults in our lives. We need them to feed us, clothe us, shelter us, and love us. And in our innocence we really don't know how to judge whether they are truly trustworthy. Instead of being who we really can be, we take on masks like The Good Little Girl or The Good Little Boy, or we become The Black Sheep of the Family or The Rebel. There are, of course, many possibilities. But the point is that early on we get the point— that if we are to be loved and cared for we'd better buckle under and be what is safe for us to be within the family dynamic.

After we have the mask self set in place, we have our position in the family system staked out. With our Black Sheep mask in place, for example, we become the recipient of all that's wrong with the family. Others don't have to own their dark side because we have been defined as the Black Sheep and will act it out for them. Furthermore, we'll continue to be valued as long as we agree to play that role. As long as we wear our Black Sheep mask, we have a place in the family.*

Eventually there comes the time when we move outside the family unit. In the world people have different needs. Not everyone will value our Black Sheep mask; indeed, people want only to push us away or try to control our behavior. Lovers, teachers, employers, the police will all try to make us over. Most will attempt to train us to be a Good Little Child instead. Maybe they'll even succeed! Ironically, whether they are successful or not, we are still invisible. We still haven't embraced who we really are.

As we struggle with our masks, often many layers must be peeled away. In the meantime life becomes a melodrama, a soap opera as we find ourselves drawn to this person or that, all in an effort to make our lives work and still hold onto our masks. For a while we may be able to get someone to play the game with us: the person with a Rescuer mask hooks up with the Maiden in Distress mask; the person with Victim Mask hooks up with the Abuser Mask, and so on.

Through these dances we play out the insanity of our lives. But each time we play and lose we're forced to look a little

---

* An excellent resource for exploring masks and inner world characters is *Embracing Our Selves: The Voice Dialogue Manual,* by Hal and Sidra Stone (Novato, CA: Nataraj, 1993).

more closely at ourselves, to ask what all our challenges are trying to mirror back to us. And bit by bit we dare to lift a corner of the mask and peek under it. If we're lucky there are times when we're caught off guard, without our masks, and at those moments of epiphany—through our peak experiences or essential wounds—we perhaps catch a glimpse of a truth bigger than the mask. If we have enough of these, and if we get to the point that we're no longer willing to suffer the perils of wearing the mask, we begin pursuing the larger truth.

The true self behind the mask—and beyond the great cast of characters we call our inner world—knows that our true nature is spiritual and is able to see beyond the Mickey Mouse suits. The true self knows that beyond the mask self each of us brings to the world, *mankind is one.*

My friend Phil, who is a psychiatrist but also a spiritual teacher, says, "The illusions of separation we experience are only that—illusions. It is impossible not to be *at one.* Whatever we experience to the contrary can only be of our own making."

What I think he means is that we create illusions of separation through our masks and our life dramas are little more than the playing out of these illusions. Yet, at the same time these dramas are very much a source of our passions and our creativity. We needn't look for anything else to fill the pages of our books. To focus in on these personal truths, to dare look closely at our masks and the inner worlds beneath them, is the way we come back to ourselves, not only to our spiritual essence but to the stories we must live through along the way.

The dramas we play out through our masks are, after all, part of our life history. They make up the legends of our life journey, and certainly there is the enigma of truth reflected in them. The masks we wear, the characters we find peopling our inner world, the dramas we play out in the external world all provide us with unlimited themes, anecdotes, and illustrations to say virtually anything we may wish to say—in fiction, non-fiction, poetry, or drama. By using this material we benefit twice: first, in the passion we bring to our writing, and second, by showing us the path back to our true selves.

11: Beyond the Mystic Circle of the Storyteller

The most beautiful thing we can experience is the mysterious. It is the source of all true art and science.

ALBERT EINSTEIN

When I was in my late twenties, I spent several months doing dream work with a Freudian psychotherapist. For the first five or six weeks, the work we did was by the book, with the therapist interpreting my dream imagery in a fairly traditional way. Everything I dreamed seemed to symbolize conflicts with mother or repressed aggression toward father. Although this was interesting, I began to notice something else in my dreams, something beyond the symbolic. As I increased the discipline of keeping a notebook at my bedside and waking to record my dreams, I noticed that much of the time my nocturnal voyages were like stories. They often had beginnings, middles, and ends. They had integral characters and even, at times, intriguing story lines, plots, or settings.

In one of the first complete dreams I was able to accurately recall and record, I was sitting in a theater, which had a round stage in the middle of a round room. The theater was packed, with the audience seated in seven circles of seats around the stage. I sat in the second row in the best section. It seemed that I was both a spectator and a cast member. I had a telephone with which I could be in constant communication with the actors as they played their parts. The actors wore headsets with tiny microphones so that we could talk back and forth as they performed. A spotlight was on me, signaling the audience that I also had a role in the play, though I spoke lines the audience could hear only twice—once at the beginning of the play, when I introduced the actors, and once at the end, when I delivered a closing monologue. I remembered the closing line very well, because it was derived from Shakespeare: "We are all like actors, who strut and fret an hour upon the stage and then are heard no more."

The actors on the stage were all very familiar to me, and I recognized that they represented, and were playing out, various parts of myself. They were following a script, but at the same time the scripted story was being acted, I would pick up the phone, dial one actor or another, and make suggestions for things that might be said or done. These were always spur-of-the-moment innovations triggered by things that had happened on the stage, not anything we'd rehearsed or that I'd previously written. I was always aware of what we'd rehearsed and what was improvised in the moment. To add complexity to the play, the actors spoke in two languages, both of which the audience understood. There appeared to be one language for symbolic meanings and another for more literal, everyday messages.

It was an intriguing production. Usually, the action unfolding on the stage came as a complete surprise to me. And at other times, when I telephoned an actor and asked him or her to try something that was not in the script, we would all be surprised by the unexpected turn of events that resulted. Although I had only a vague memory of the basic script, the main story line seemed to be made up of fragments from a variety of Eugene O'Neill's plays, whose work I was reading at the time. As the play ended the audience applauded, and when I stood and bowed from my place offstage, the audience applauded even more. I bowed, feeling tremendously satisfied with myself.

In my next therapy session, I read the description of the dream to my therapist. I was glowing with pride. To my frustration she looked thoughtful and grave, then spent the next twenty minutes explaining that it was all about fear and my need for control. She told me that I was in the audience, as the director of any play might be, but the telephone line to the actors symbolized my unwillingness to let go and trust the actors. The actors, she said, symbolized important people in my life, and she promised that in our next sessions we could dissect my relationships with them in greater detail.

That night I considered what she had told me, and I agreed that although the dream probably did reveal something about my need for control, I also saw it as a fascinating concept for a theater piece. Because I was apprenticing in the theater at the time, I began to write a play based on the dream—with an actor in the audience with a phone and others on stage with headsets. Moreover, I devised a way for some actors to turn and speak directly to the audience while giving the illusion that the other actors weren't able to hear them. In a way, then, two languages would be represented: one that communicated within the action of the script, the other a private language between certain actors and the audience.

As an artistic piece, the idea was more ambitious than I had the skill to handle at the time, so I eventually shelved it.

But what came out of this experience was the realization that our dreams really are a tremendous creative wellspring. There may be layers and layers of symbolic meaning to be mined for psychotherapy, but on a more obvious level we should also learn to appreciate our dreams as, quite literally, creative brainstorms. Since that day I have always looked to my dreams for ideas that might be developed into stories, articles, new forms, characters, or nonfiction book ideas.

Many years after I left psychotherapy, I became interested in shamanism and the use of dance and ritual in early societies. What intrigued me was that shamans often drew their wisdom not only from tradition and direct experience but also from what parapsychologists and mystics call the invisible reality. The shaman believes there is a reality that parallels our physical lives but that we cannot hear, see, smell, taste, or touch—a world outside our five senses. Those of us who were raised within the scientific tradition are taught that what we cannot perceive through our senses does not exist. And, of course, there is much debate, even in the scientific community, about what's real and what's not.

Within most shamanic traditions, dreamtime is believed to be the way we access the wisdom of the invisible reality. Through active imagination, hallucinogens, ritual, drumming, and dance, shamans enter an altered state of consciousness. In this state they may see themselves not just as witnesses of their dreams but as participants. And from their journeys in the other world they bring back visions and teachings to assist their tribes in making changes, be it in finding new hunting territories, healing personal relationships, or bringing greater balance and harmony between the tribe and the natural order.

Often, shamans' wisdom was communicated to others through storytelling. Members of the community would sit in a circle, and storytellers would tell their stories, very often acting out various parts, seeming to take on the guise of another person, an animal, or a god. The stories were always seen as coming from the invisible reality. Even when storytellers repeated one of the more traditional stories, for example, stories of Coyote the Trickster, they would virtually reinterpret the old tales every time they were performed.

Although several years had passed between when I had the theater dream and when I became interested in shamanism, I remembered the dream and went to the journal where I'd recorded it. I was immediately surprised at the similarities between that dream and certain shamanic practices. I was initially impressed by the similarity between my theater in the round and the traditional medicine wheel of indigenous societies. The medicine wheel is, in effect, a group of people gathering in a circle. In the circle each person brings his or her voice to the center, in response to a problem the community may be having. Out of the synergy of the total group's participation comes a new direction or vision of the problem. In that respect, no one person is considered to have the final solution; rather, it is believed that the Great Spirit moves through each person, and each contributes his or her small piece of the total picture. Only when the total activity of the medicine wheel is viewed as a whole do we have anything resembling an understanding of the issue.

Often, the stories of the shamans or other storytellers, which originated in the dream space, would establish the theme, as it were, for the medicine wheel. Ultimately, then, there was complete interaction between a storyteller and the other people sitting in the circle. The story, drawn from the dream space, literally entered the consciousness of the spectators, perhaps triggering ideas or visions that would then be fed back to the circle when those spectators spoke or in some other way took an active part in the circle, like telling another story, dancing, drumming, or simply speaking their mind.

Those early storytellers were deeply involved with the invisible reality—which today would be called our emotional and spiritual life. They saw life as a constant interweaving between the physical world and the other reality that exists outside the reach of the five senses. They believed their work on the physical plane was relatively straightforward, consisting of learning how to feed, clothe, and shelter themselves and their families and developing positive relationships with their communities. The more difficult work was encountered in their relationship to the invisible reality, that is, honoring the spiritual life and their relationship to the universe.

As storytellers, then, their work was not aimless recreation but a way of giving the invisible reality form in the physical world. The story drawn from dreamtime invariably brought a message that helped storyteller and spectator alike better understand their relationship with the spiritual life. What's perhaps even more important to see is that when those stories were performed, there was very hot participation with the spectator. Storytellers would respond to their listeners, just as live entertainers respond to their audiences today. It seemed that in working together, storyteller and listeners pumped the deep, inner wisdom from the conduit the storyteller had set up with the invisible reality.

When the printing press came into widespread use, it created a separation between the writer and the reader (or listener) that was absent in the days of the early storytellers. Today, with the printed word, the author has little or no contact with the reader, and the pump provided by the synergy between storyteller and listener has almost disappeared. After all, readers are not present during the actual performance, that is, the writing, thus limiting their impact on the creative process. Still, writers must draw from the invisible reality—the dreams, the visions, the memories, and imaginings that come out of their life experiences.

The invisible world, the world of imagination and dream, is filled with mystery and is rich with creative resources, so as writers we should take advantage of any opportunity to draw from it. But to maximize our use, we need to get away from dream interpretation. Although I think there is much to learn from dreams about our emotions, my sense is that as writers we make full use of this tremendous resource only when we honor the mystery and allow the other reality to tell us its stories. Instead of attempting to interpret the hidden language of the other reality, take the stories and characters whole. Always remember they are much more than the symbolic interpretations you may impose on them. Play them out on the page by telling a story or following a theme you may have recognized in them. And finally, when you write pretend you're a storyteller sitting with a group around a campfire at night. Imagine the live presentation of your material and its affects on the other people in the circle. Respond to their cheers, to their oohs and ahhs by shifting your story slightly, embellishing it here and there for a deeper affect.

It's all too easy for modern writers to forget that we can and do have an impact on thousands of people. The realities we create on the page enter into readers' lives, in some cases radically changing them. That's something we would immediately understand if we were working in the oral tradition, telling stories to a circle of our community members; it's something we frequently lose sight of when we're telling our stories for the printed page. There is a mystical connection between writer and reader that needs to be honored, one that skeptics may challenge but that is increasingly difficult to deny.

As a writer, I have been fascinated by the emerging new sciences that recognize the existence of the invisible reality beyond the reach of our five senses. And it is particularly interesting to note, as Joseph Campbell does, that as technology has evolved to the point of allowing us to send astronauts to outer space, we are awed more than ever by what we find in our voyages beyond the earth's atmosphere. Campbell makes the point that "the voyages into outer space turn us back to inner space."

Brian O'Leary, an astronomer and NASA scientist-astronaut during the Apollo program and deputy team leader of the Mariner 10 television science team, writes:

> The new reality presumes an interconnectedness, a higher order in the universe that cannot be explained simply by known physical laws. It observes the power of the mind. . . . It considers dimensions beyond time and space, concepts beyond matter and energy as currently understood, and realms beyond the physical.

We are not, by any means, the first generation to recognize the existence of the other reality. Jung, for example, explored it about as thoroughly and scientifically as anyone has in recent history. In fact, toward the end of his life he attributed much of the success of his intellectual efforts and his writings to experiences he had with inner guides. These were disembodied entities that emerged from his deep unconscious mind; the best known was Philemon, whose counsel Jung consistently called upon throughout his life. He described Philemon, as well as other "fantasy" figures through whom he received information, in the following way:

Philemon represented superior insight. He was a mysterious figure to me. At times he seemed to me quite real, as if he was a living personality. I went walking up and down the garden with him, and he was what the Indians call a guru.

Jung believed the fantasy figures had an identity separate from his mind. He stated that his experiences with Philemon and other figures brought home to him the "crucial insight that there are things in the psyche which I do not produce, but which produce themselves and have their own life." He believed, like so many students of the new science, that at least part of the psyche is not subject to what we presently perceive as the limits of time and space. He stated that "the psyche at times functions outside of the spatio-temporal law of causality."

In recent years, there has been an increasing interest in channeling, whereby a person is able to make contact with an entity or disembodied soul from "the other side." The best known of these are Jane Roberts "Seth" channelings; the channeling of *A Course In Miracles,* by the psychologist Helen Schucman; and the work of Kevin Ryerson, popularized by Shirley MacLaine. When we look at these writings, we find bits of quite extraordinary wisdom, often beyond the range of the channel's study and education. It seems that regardless of the explanation for this practice, the authors were able somehow to create what amounts to a psychic conduit from their everyday realities to realities that cannot be easily explained in conventional terms.

The practice of creating a certain character unlike ourselves or of assuming a character from another source, such as a legendary hero or a religious figure, goes as far back in history as we can trace. I mentioned one example in the previous chapter—the story about the little girl's remark about the kachina dancers. Most early societies held dances and other ceremonies, in which people would don the costume and mask of a deity. In doing so, they literally took on the character of that figure and lost their identities. When fully in character, dancers under the mask seemed to disappear, saying and doing things that appeared to be quite beyond their capacities in their everyday state of mind. This, too, was a form of channeling.

I know of no satisfactory explanation for what happens when we assume characters other than ours and use them as ways of accessing information from other psychic dimensions. But it is clear to me that it is a wonderful addition to one's creative process. At the very least, I have to agree with Arthur Hastings, Ph.D., whose book *Tongues of Men and Angels: A Study of Channeling* is without a doubt the most responsible and exhaustive treatment of this phenomenon in print today. In that book he concludes:

> We do not have enough understanding of the mind and its reaches to say with certainty what is possible and what is not. Our beliefs should be open to change as we learn more. We can still come to conclusions for practical purposes and test their value by how useful they are in understanding experience and guiding action. The models we use should be steppingstones for further exploration.

Techniques for developing these characters vary widely, from immersing yourself in a figure from history, to asking for a guide to come to you in your dreams, to entering an altered state through deep meditation and asking for a figure to come to you for help with an issue or writing problem. In chapter five I spoke of Awahakeewah, a spirit guide to whom I often turn for guidance in writing. That guide came to me initially when I was still in high school. During a hunting trip in northern Michigan I sat under a tree, and in the process of trying to make myself comfortable I reached under my right buttock to remove what I thought was a sharp rock. Instead, my hand curled around what turned out to be a beautifully sculpted tomahawk head, several hundred years old.

Some years later I was holding the tomahawk head while meditating. As I moved deeper and deeper into meditation, a figure of a native American began to form in my mind. It was a vivid image and, like Jung, I was somewhat startled because he seemed very real to me, not like a character I'd create for a story. Awahakeewah explained that he had been the owner of the tomahawk head and that he had also been a toolmaker for his community. His lecture to me about the Creative Spirit, which I recorded in chapter five, has continued to have a strong influence on me, and I often turn to him for guidance whenever I have trouble in that area. My work with Awahakeewah has convinced me there is another dimension of reality, much greater than our firsthand experience of the world, and that we probably have access to it at all times, though we don't often make use of it in the modern world where we have learned to discount such beliefs on scientific grounds.

Jon Klimo, interdisciplinary researcher and author of *Channeling: Investigations on Receiving Information from Paranormal Sources,* theorizes the following:

> Perhaps God, the Universe, or All-That-Exists, is really something like a dissociated Being, a multiple personality, as experienced from our perspective as Its own dissociated subpersonalities. All aspects of Creation are in an evolutionary process of overcoming this "cosmological dissociation." As

part of this overcoming process, we are learning to transmute our condition of relative disconnectedness and to access ever more of the omniscience, omnipotence, omnipresence, and omnibenevolence of our common Universal Being. Unfortunately, at this stage of our evolution, much of the energy and information involved in such accessing is being condescendingly perceived as somehow sub-real or unreal, as only imaginational, delusional, mystical, magical, or paranormal in nature, whereas it is in actuality manifestations of a deeper truth and a greater reality.

I urge every writer I meet to consider the possibility that there is a reality much greater than ourselves, one that is not limited by time, space, the five senses, or any of the physical laws we understand. Moreover, we are inexplicably at-one with this greater reality, not cut off from it by the outer layer of skin and bone that defines our physical bodies. We awaken to this reality and draw from it for our creative inspiration, not by sequestering ourselves away in the proverbial garret to do our writing, burdened by the belief that we are all alone in the creative act, but by opening ourselves to the possibility that we may be able to ask for and get assistance from it. This can be done through a channeled inner guide or by live readings so we can experience the power of the synergy between author and listener that the ancient oral storytellers knew so well, or through prayer, or by entering altered states of consciousness from a variety of means. The act of writing itself places us in a nonordinary state of consciousness, wherein this other reality is just a short journey away.

Let's go there!

12: Getting Happily Published

Even though so much of my writing time is stressful and disheartening, I carry a secret sense of accomplishment around with me, like a radium pack implanted near my heart that now leaches a quiet sense of relief through my system.

ANNE LAMOTT

While putting the finishing touches on this book, I was reminded that one of the most frequently asked questions in any group of young writers is How do I get published? The short answer is Write something that publishers want. Although that may sound flippant, there is more than a bit of truth in it. I'm always reminding myself that although most authors write to satisfy a deep inner need, most publishers publish to make money. Keeping a publishing company afloat means they have to sell books, and that means that they must develop a good eye for manuscripts that are going to stir up some excitement in the marketplace. As authors we should be grateful that somebody is looking out for the money end of publishing. God knows writers aren't very good at that.

Don't get me wrong. I don't think writers should write what they think publishers or even their readers want. On the contrary! If there's one ingredient publishers look for in that stack of manuscripts that comes in over the transom every month, it has something to do with how deeply authors are enmeshed in their works. When the author is passionately involved, that passion comes across with every word, and it excites readers. In that respect, we could probably draw some parallels between writing and making love. There's nothing quite so gloomy as trying to do either with a partner whose heart isn't in it.

When I started getting published I asked an editor from a large New York publishing house what she looked for in a manuscript. She told me, "I'm looking for writing that comes from the heart, books that are written because the author *has* to write them. If that deep involvement is there, I'll work with the author until we produce something that's publishable. I don't care what the subject is as long as this rare ingredient is present."

I'm not sure every publisher thinks this way, but there's more than a little truth in the editor's words. Good acquisitions editors keep an eye focused on current trends, but they also know it's impossible to predict what's going to be a bestseller a year from now, which is about the shortest time it will take the writer and publisher to produce a book. Knowing that nobody has clear vision when it comes to predicting what's going to sell next year, the smart editors look for a new idea and the author's passion.

Why is the author's passion for the material so important? I contend it's for the same reason that magazines like *People* and *Us* are so popular—that we all take a kind of voyeuristic delight in looking at the world through another person's eyes.

It's not just that we're curious about how others live. What we really want is to get outside ourselves and look at life in a different way. We want to get over ourselves, to perhaps discover and enjoy a part of life we had overlooked. Readers are generally voracious about wanting to get more out of life, and it's then the author's passion draws us in like a powerful magnet.

All this is well and good, but the next question is How do I get a publisher to even look at my manuscript? The truth is that most of the large publishers—houses like Random House, Doubleday, Harper, Simon & Schuster—won't look at unsolicited manuscripts. That's shorthand for I'll look only at manuscripts brought to me by literary agents. And what do they do with the unsolicited ones? I got a wonderful object lesson nearly twenty years ago when I flew to New York to meet with an editor at one of the largest publishing houses in the city.

I took the elevator to the tenth floor, and when the doors opened I found myself facing a bored receptionist, barely visible behind a large pile of manuscripts. She took my name, repeated it into her intercom, and told me to take a seat. Meanwhile, she opened the big envelopes on her desk, flipped through them, then stuffed them into other envelopes and tossed them into a plastic mail container on the floor. I guess she riffled through the pages of every fifth or sixth manuscript. I asked her,

"What's in all those envelopes?"

"Manuscripts people send," she replied, listlessly. "We get a whole stack of them every day."

"Are you the main person who reads them?" I asked.

"I don't really read them," she said. "Sometimes I glance through one or two if they look interesting."

"And what makes a manuscript *look interesting*?"

"Oh, I don't know. Sometimes a title. Sometimes just the fact that it's nicely printed out. I can't really say."

I was speechless. I thought about all the manuscripts I'd sent before I had an agent. And I quickly calculated how much money I had contributed to the U.S. Postal Service, to say nothing of the copy services near my home, in order to have this person, or her counterpart, go through her little ritual. Roughly estimating the number of freelance writers in America who have no agents, I concluded that their contribution alone could support pensions for the entire postal service!

Finding an Agent

The next most logical question is How do I get an agent so that my work can move beyond the status of the unsolicited manuscript? And the answer to that is the same I gave to the question How do I get published? only more. People become successful agents for one reason only: They consistently deliver to publishers manuscripts that require minimal editing and sell well after they're made into books. Agents are salespeople; they need products—your book—to sell.

Now comes another frustration to make you a little more crazy than you already are: The chances are that agents who've been around for a while are going to tell you they don't look at authors who haven't previously published. So you're down in the sand trap again because you haven't been published before . . . and if you had been you probably wouldn't be worrying about how to get an agent.

I said that *successful agents who've been around for a while* don't take on unpublished authors. However, that's just one category of agents. The other category is the agent who is just starting out and is looking desperately for some *good properties* to handle. These folks are in a position very similar to yours: They want to be agents but all the successful published authors already have agents. So they need you as much as you need them. And just because they're new in the business doesn't mean they can't do a good job for you, any more than your not being published yet means you're not a good writer.

Most literary agents are people who have worked in publishing, usually as editors, and they've built up some good contacts and know how to get a foot in the door of at least a couple of major publishers. They lost their jobs through downsizing of the company or because somebody didn't like them, or they got sick and tired of working long hours in-house for too little pay and want to be their own bosses. How do you meet them? If you live in or near a large city, you will probably know of a writers' club or a place where writers' workshops are given. Agents who are just starting frequent such places looking for new clients. So keep an eye out for them: they may present a class on publishing or simply announce their presence at regular meetings. They may even be members of writers' clubs, which they join in order to scout for new clients.

You will also find listings for literary agents in two key writers' reference guides: *Literary Market Place* (LMP) and Writer's Digest Books' annual *Guide to Literary Agents*. Both sources provide descriptions of agents, the genres they specialize in, whether they take on new writers, and, of course, where they can be reached.

I'd also highly recommend subscribing to *Publishers Weekly*, which is essentially the publishing industry's house organ. There's no better way to educate yourself to what's really

going on in publishing and the world of the literary agent. This
is where you get all the inside information on what publishers,
editors, agents are doing—plus short reviews of the newest
books, interviews with authors, forecasts of what's coming up,
and the ubiquitous best-seller lists. In the back of each weekly
magazine you'll also find classified ads and an occasional notice of new literary agencies starting. Reading it each week
can be maddening—particularly when you hear about the lat-
est multimillion dollar advance to a romance novelist who
you're certain isn't half as deserving as you are.

The best way to approach an agent is with a short query
letter describing your project. By short I mean one page with
one paragraph describing your book and a second telling a little about yourself. For example, if you are writing a book on a
medical subject, give your medical credentials or tell about a
coauthor who has credentials. If your book is a novel or a collection of poems, then formal credentials probably will not be
as relevant. Don't make the mistake of getting too chatty and
cute, either; agents really don't care if you have a bull terrier
named Sherwood (Anderson) or a Persian cat named Zelda
who snuggles on top of your monitor when you write.

In your cover letter, avoid hyping either your book or yourself. One of the banes of every agent is having to deal with
temperamental authors and their overblown egos. Too much
hype in a cover letter is like waving a red flag. So stick to business and get to the point quickly and cleanly. Query letters are
important, and there's an art to writing really good ones. For
further help, consult books on writing query letters, one of
which you'll find cited in the Bibliography.

Most publishers and agents tend to specialize in particular
kinds of books. For example, some publishers want to see only

mystery novels. Others want to see only nonfiction, perhaps biographies and popular sociology. Do some research before you send queries. Make certain you send letters to people who work with the genre in which you're writing. Again, browse *Literary Market Place, Writer's Market,* and listings of agents.

One of the best ways for a beginning writer to get an agent or a publisher is to be referred by a friend who is a published writer. But not all of us can boast of having such a person in our collection of friends. Regardless, keep your eyes open for any opportunity to make a connection with other writers who might be interested in your project. For example, let's say you take a workshop from an author who is writing on something similar to your topic. After you've taken the class and know the author a bit, simply ask for an agent or publisher recommendation. Also ask if he or she would consider taking a look at your manuscript, with the possibility of giving you a referral to his or her agent or publisher. Most authors are open to this; others make it their policy never to stick their necks out. But don't be afraid to ask.

About Book Proposals

In the past twenty years, most nonfiction books have been sold to publishers on the basis of a selling proposal. This is a description of your book, presented in what has become a fairly standardized format. (See Bibliography, *How To Write a Book Proposal.*) Publishers give advances against royalties based on these proposals, giving authors the financial resources they'll need to complete their manuscripts. Advances run from a few hundred dollars into the millions, depending on the potential salability of the finished project.

First-time fiction writers don't sell books on the basis of a proposal, however, although I'll never say never. Still, if you're a fiction writer, count on presenting a finished manuscript to your agent. After you've had a couple of best-sellers, you can probably talk to your publisher about an advance based on a new book idea.

The Status of Writers

Most of us who still have a reverence for books also think of authors as special people. Even a minor poet in a small town can be a celebrity. But within big-time publishing, the author is just one cog in the complex gearing of a very complicated machine. The day you turn over your final draft to your editor, a chain of activities is set into motion using acquisitions editors (your main contact with the publisher), line editors, copy editors, publicity and marketing people, the accounting department, book designers, a cover artist, typesetters, binderies, warehouse workers, the catalog department, sales representatives, booksellers, and, finally, way down the line, readers. As difficult as it may be to accept, you are just the supplier of the raw material for a product these people will shape into the product called a book.

It's important for authors to keep some perspective. Give the other people who will be involved with your book proper credit. Recognize that without their help you would never get into print. A little humility, patience, and a show of appreciation will go a long way. Eight years ago I had a publishing experience that truly humbled me. My editor at one of New York's largest publishing houses called me one afternoon to share the following story. She was going to her office after lunch when she dropped by the publicity department and saw a huge stack of my new books, which were being mailed to reviewers. Because she had not yet received a copy, she asked the publicist if she could have one.

"Not on your life," the publicist said. "These are all earmarked for our reviewers' list."

Somewhat miffed, my editor sputtered, "Are editors the last ones to get copies?"

The publicist glanced at the ceiling, looked thoughtful, then replied: "No. I believe the authors are."

I don't think there was any hostility in this answer. The publicist was just stating a fact. Remember, few people who work on the editing and publishing of a book ever see or even talk to the author. They talk with each other and with their coworkers, but the author simply doesn't exist as a real person for them. Authors seldom visit their publishers, and in all the years I've been writing I have never had an editor introduce me to anyone else in the house—even when I went there to visit. In fact, I would not recognize most editors of the more than two hundred books I've been involved with. Particularly when a publisher is across the country, your only contact with editors will be by phone or by letter. And by the way, editors don't win any awards for returning phone calls.

In the broad scheme of things, it's important to see where we writers fit in. Even though the industry is dependent on the raw material we provide, we're also only semivisible to most of the people who do what's necessary to transform our manuscripts into books and get them into the marketplace. If we're to be happily published, we need to know how to stick up for ourselves, but we also need to give credit where it's due. It means sending signed copies of your book, with a short note of appreciation, to your editor and all the other people you've had contact with in the process of getting your work out. And it also means joining a writers' union such as the Author's Guild (see Bibliography), which can act as your advocate in those rare times when you will need one.

The New Independents*

In the past twenty years there have been some major changes in book publishing that all new writers should understand before submitting manuscripts. The best way to describe these changes is to look at the publisher of this book. Nataraj is a good example of what has come to be known in the industry as an independent publisher.

The company was started by Shakti Gawain and her husband, Jim Burns, who wanted a way to publish not only Shakti's books, which were already best-sellers, but to take on book projects they felt could be helpful to people committed to a path of personal and spiritual development. In this respect, Nataraj's focus is a broad one, its core readership being people who know and are attracted to Shakti's work as well as authors of similar backgrounds and interests. With Shakti's books selling in the millions, the readership this company serves is indeed a large one.

---

*I have just learned about *The Heart of Independent Publishing*, to be published in 1996 by Wildcat Canyon Press in Berkeley, California, edited by Julienne Bennett (no relation), co-publisher of *50 Simple Things You Can Do to Save the Earth*. The book includes interviews with many hightly successful independent publishers. Call the publisher for further information: 510-848-3600.

In today's publishing world, independent publishers are a significant force. They can be small (one or two books per year) or large (a dozen or more books per year) operations serving authors and a readership that for the most part have been abandoned by the large New York publishing houses. To understand why this is so, one should know a little about publishing history. So let's go back a bit.

Until the late 1960s, most New York publishing houses were family run and existed with narrow profit margins. Editorial policies were very loose. These houses published what personally appealed to their publishers or their editors. If a book sold only three thousand copies but made an important statement, it was considered a success. Then, larger conglomerates, mainly Hollywood and New York media interests, started buying book publishers, and at this point the bottom line, and turning a good profit, became more important than publishing quality work. Today, New York publishing is best-seller driven and every editor is looking for best-sellers first and message books or good literature second.

When New York started chasing after best-sellers, some excellent books went begging. As a result, the industry suddenly broke off onto a new path—giving rise to the small, independent publisher usually controlled by one person, much as New York publishing was in its infancy.

In the beginning the new independents had a hard time. They were acquiring and publishing excellent material, but they lacked the distribution channels to get their products into the marketplace. To answer this need, independent distributors began cropping up throughout the country, companies like Book People, New Leaf, and The Great Tradition.

These distributors handled mostly small, independent publishers. They provided cataloging and shipping services, and got the books into stores. But most distributors were local businesses, serving bookstores in one or two states. They also lacked book reps, that is, salespeople who went into the stores, talked to booksellers, checked how their books were being displayed, and got their products recognized. Most independent distributors and publishers depended on booksellers ordering from catalogs, which were simply alphabetized lists of different publishers' offerings.

In the 1980s independent distributors went a step further, building into their lists of services sales representatives who made personal contact with booksellers, advised independent publishers on how to better promote their books, began advertising in trade journals, and offered cataloging that served publishers and booksellers in ways comparable to the big New York publishers. Today, this brand of book distributor has made it possible for niche publishers to compete with even the biggest New York publishers. What's more, the best of the independents are now producing books that are themselves best-sellers, that is, single titles that sell in the hundreds of thousands or even millions of copies, just like their giant New York counterparts.

For the beginning writer, the new independents are generally more approachable than the larger New York houses. Most will read unsolicited manuscripts, and many prefer dealing directly with authors rather than going through agents. In addition, they provide more personal help. On the downside, most independents don't have the big budgets that the larger houses do, so don't expect a huge advance. But there are tradeoffs that can more than make up for the difference, particularly for writers who haven't yet established a track record. Because they must have something to attract writers, the independents offer more personal contact with their authors, giving editorial help similar to what New York houses gave in the 1920s and 1930s. People in publishing tend to forget that the era of the great American novel, when literary giants such as Ernest Hemingway, F. Scott Fitzgerald, Katherine Ann Porter, William Faulkner, Lillian Hellman, and Sherwood Anderson came along there were also some gifted editors, notably Maxwell Perkins, who helped those authors. Although it is rare for a large New York house to put a lot of effort into developing their authors, the tradition of the developmental editor is still very much alive with many independents.

Besides offering editorial support, the independent publisher tends to get books out a little quicker than do the larger houses. An efficient independent can produce a book within six months of receiving a finished manuscript; a larger house takes up to a year and a half. What this means is that your book starts earning money for you up to a year sooner.

Another selling point to consider is that independent publishers must make every book count. They buy books that will "backlist." What this means is that they will keep books in their catalogs for a long time—ten years or more, in many cases. For example, *The Well Body Book* was published by a small independent called Bookworks and was distributed through Random House in New York. In its first year the book sold twenty thousand copies. But it stayed in print for ten years, getting into print in several other countries, for total sales of more than a quarter-million copies. With a larger New York house it might or might not have stayed in print so long.

About Publicity

I think all published writers complain that their publishers don't do enough to promote their books. We all blame our publishers when our treasured works didn't become best-sellers. But the truth is that the best advertising for any book is itself. Books are probably the most word-of-mouth product in the world. Although there are exceptions, a book sells because its readers are excited about it and want their friends to read it, too. Readers broadcast their enthusiasm and this, more than anything else, sells books.

Print advertising is expensive. To earn back the cost of one ad in the *New York Times,* publishers must sell nearly a thousand books. However, one ad barely gets recognized. So if they're going to make it work at all they have to buy at least six ads, and that's big money. They'll have to sell five thousand books to earn back just the advertising budget. Considering that the average book sells only about five thousand copies, advertising simply isn't an economically practical way to promote books. There's a joke in the publishing world that really isn't a joke—that the only books that get any promotion to speak of are books that don't need it, books by celebrity authors or novelists whose books sell in the hundreds of thousands with or without advertising.

What does work then? How do books find their way to their readers? A standard promotion for most publishers consists of sending books to book reviewers for newspapers and magazines throughout the country. A reviewers' list can include 150 to 500 individuals, depending on the subject matter. In addition, your publisher usually sends press releases to radio and TV broadcasters, hoping that some will be interested enough in your work either to interview you or to have you on their programs as a guest. Aside from that, your publisher should make certain that the book rep, that is, the person who goes out and takes orders from booksellers, knows about your book. Publishers have sales conferences for this, an insiders' event that authors are rarely invited to attend. And finally, they display your book at either the American Booksellers Association, the big annual publishing event attended by thousands of publishers and booksellers, or at regional bookseller associations throughout the country. A picture and a description of your book will also be in the publisher's catalog, the catalogs of distributors they may use, or both.

The most powerful promotion of all however, comes from you. For example, more and more booksellers are developing ongoing instore programs for authors to speak directly to customers and, they hope, sign a stack of books that authors will help sell. You and your book will be advertised through the store and probably through the local newspapers. Readers love the opportunity to meet their favorite authors in person. You can always start your publicity by making contact with owners of your local bookstores. Although most publishers will help you with all the details and will make certain there are books in stock for your appearance, your personal contact with the bookseller is one of the greatest assets you have.

If your book lends itself to lectures or workshops, use these, one of the best avenues of promotion. People will pay to attend functions such as these, and many authors make more money this way than they do selling books. The best thing about it is that you get paid for doing something that is good advertising for your book! For lectures, think of everything from service clubs to writers workshops, wherever your book can fit in. Self-promotion of this kind can be a gold mine for writers who are willing to put themselves out there.

It's important for beginning writers to keep some perspective about writing. Publishing will probably not change your life. Few writers become rich or famous in today's world. But there are rewards here that you will find in few other professions. So, it is a golden grail definitely worth pursuing, with compensations that feed not just your pocketbook or your ego, but something much more important—your very soul.

Bibliography

Introduction

Fox, Matthew. *The Reinvention of Work: A New Vision of Livelihood for Our Time.* San Francisco, HarperCollins: 1994.

Chapter 1

Csikszentmihalyi, Mihaly. *Flow: The Psychology of Optimal Experience.* New York, Harper Perennial: 1991.

The New Oxford English Bible. Cambridge, Oxford University Press: 1970.

Kuhlewind, Georg, *Becoming Aware of the Logos.* New York, The Lindisfarne Press: 1985.

Chapter 2

Stevens, Wallace, *The Necessary Angel:* 1951.

Bennett, Hal Zina, and Samuels, Michael. *The Well Body Book.* New York, Random House-Bookworks: 1972.

Chapter 3

Wordsworth, William, "I Wandered Lonely as a Cloud": 1807.

Whitehead, Alfred North, "Adventures of Ideas": 1933.

Chapter 4

Emerson, Ralph Waldo, "Self Reliance": 1847.

Bennett, Hal Zina. *No More Public School.* New York, Random House-Bookworks: 1971.

Hemingway, Ernest, "Paris Review," Spring 1958.

Chapter 5

Osbon, Diane K. ed., *A Joseph Campbell Companion.* New York, HarperCollins: 1991.

Chapter 6
Browning, Robert, "Saul": 1855.
Keller, Helen, *The Story of My Life*. New York, Putnam: 1902.

Chapter 7
Krishnamurti, J., *Meeting Life*. New York, HarperCollins: 1991.
Stevens, Wallace, "Peter Quince at the Clavier": 1947.

Chapter 8
Jung, C.G., recorded and edited by Aniela Jaffe, *Memories, Dreams, Reflections*. New York, Vintage Books: 1965.

Chapter 9
Campbell, Joseph, *An Open Life*. Burdett, New York, Larsen Publications: 1988.
Faulkner, William, "Nobel Prize Acceptance Speech," December 10, 1950.
Mueller, Gertrud, *Here All Dwell Free*. New York, Doubleday: 1991.

Chapter 10
Csikszentmihalyi, Mihaly, *Flow: The Psychology of Optimal Experience*. New York, Harper Perennial: 1991.
Stone, Hal and Sidra, *Embracing Our Selves: The Voice Dialogue Manual*. Novato, California, Nataraj: 1993.

Chapter 11
Einstein, Albert. *What I Believe*. Boston, Houghton Mifflin: 1930.
Kennedy, Eugene, "Earthwise: The Dawning of a New Spiritual Awareness." An interview with Joseph Campbell. The *New York Times* Magazine, April 15, 1979.
O'Leary, Brian, *Exploring Inner and Outer Space*. Berkeley, California, North Atlantic Books: 1989.
Jung, C.G., *Memories, Dreams, Reflections*. Recorded and edited by Aniela Jaffe. New York, Vintage Books: 1965.

Hastings, Arthur, *With the Tongues of Men and Angels.* New York, Holt, Rinehart and Winston: 1991.

Klimo, Jon, *Channeling: Investigations on Receiving Information from Paranormal Sources.* Los Angeles, Tarcher Books: 1987.

"Cosmological Dissociation." By Jon Klimo. Proceedings of the Second International Conference on Paranormal Research, Fort Collins, Colorado: 1989.

Chapter 12

Lamott, Anne, *Bird by Bird.* New York, Pantheon Books: 1994.

Literary Market Place (annual), Bowker Publications, New York.

Guide to Literary Agents (annual), Writer's Digest Books, Cincinnati, Ohio.

Cool, Lisa Collier, *How to Write Irresistible Query Letters.* Cincinnati, Ohio, Writer's Digest Books: 1991.

"Publishers Weekly," 249 West 17th Street, New York, N.Y. 10011.

Writer's Market. (annual) Cincinnati, Ohio, Writer's Digest Books.

Larsen, Michael, *How To Write a Book Proposal.* Cincinnati, Ohio, Writer's Digest Books: 1985.

The Authors Guild, Inc., 330 West 42nd Street, New York, N.Y. 10036, phone (212) 563-5904 / fax (212) 564-5363.

Bennett, Julienne, and Roy Carlisle, *The Heart of Independent Publishing: An Independent Guide for Independent Presses.* Berkeley, California, Wildcat Canyon Press: 1996.

About Hal Zina Bennett

Hal Zina Bennett began his writing career in 1970 with the publication of *The Well Body Book,* a pioneering work that helped launch the field of self-help/holistic health, now a major publishing category. He is one of the original stable of writers from the legendary Bookworks-Random House venture of the early 1970s, which helped put West Coast publishing on the map.

Hal has since authored more than twenty successful books and now consults for several of the country's leading independent publishers. In addition to writing his own books he is one of the most sought-after collaborative writers and shaping editors in the country. He has helped more than 200 authors develop their projects for today's highly competitive book industry.

Hal graduated from the creative writing program at San Francisco State University, where he studied novel-writing with award-winning authors Walter Van Tilburg Clark (*The Oxbow Incident*), Wright Morris (*Love Among the Cannibals*), and Mark Harris (*Bang the Drums Slowly*). He taught classes and workshops at The Institute of Transpersonal Psychology, The Omega Institute, Golden Gate University, Humboldt State University, Writers' Connection, and the American River College. He teaches private writing workshops and clinics throughout the country. As a consultant he is available to authors and publishers for short- or long-term assistance.

For more information about his lectures, consulting work (for authors or publishers), workshops, and newsletter, call 1-800-738-6721.

Other Books by the Author

The Lens of Perception
Exploring the Roots of Human Consciousness

Zuni Fetishes
Using Native American Objects
for Meditation, Reflections and Insight

Follow Your Bliss
Personal Fulfillment in Your Work and Relationships

How to Write with a Collaborator
The Writer's "Bible" for Putting Together Successful
Co-Authorships, Ghost Writing Arrangements and More

Inner Guides, Visions, and Dreams
Tools for Tapping the Powers of Our Inner Resources

Mind Jogger
Intuitive Insights and Divination for Everyday Life

Peak Performance
Mental Training Techniques of the World's Greatest Athletes
(with Charles A. Garfield)

The Doctor Within
How Our Bodies Heal Themselves

The Well Body Book
Pioneering Work on Self-Help Health
(with Mike Samuels, M.D.)

The Holotropic Mind
The Three Levels of Human Consciousness
and How They Shape our Lives
(for Stanislav Grof, M.D.)

The New Dimensions Book Series
(Series Editor)
Leading thinkers, artists, scientists, and social innovators
of our time, in conversation with Michael Toms, from the
award-winning "New Dimensions Radio" series

Recommended Resources

Awakening: A Daily Guide to Conscious Living. By Shakti Gawain. A daily meditation guide that focuses on maintaining your spiritual center, not just when you are in solitude, but when you are in the world, and especially, in relationships. (Tradepaper $9.95)

The Four Levels of Healing: A Guide to Balancing the Spiritual, Mental, Emotional, and Physical Aspects of Life. By Shakti Gawain. Personal growth pioneer Shakti Gawain reveals how to find and maintain a strong connection with your spiritual source.
(Hardcover $12.95)

Living in the Light (Revised): A Guide to Personal and Planetary Transformation. By Shakti Gawain, with Laurel King. The recognized classic on developing intuition and using it as a guide in living your life. (Tradepaper $12.95)

Living in the Light Workbook (Revised). By Shakti Gawain. Following up her bestseller, *Living in the Light,* Shakti has created a workbook to help us apply these principles to our lives in very practical ways. (Tradepaper $12.95)

The Path of Transformation: How Healing Ourselves Can Change the World. By Shakti Gawain. Shakti gave us *Creative Visualization* in the '70s, *Living in the Light* in the '80, and now *The Path of Transformation* for '90s. Shakti's new bestseller delivers an inspiring and provocative message for the path of true transformation. (Tradepaper $11.95)

Return to the Garden: A Journey of Discovery. By Shakti Gawain. Shakti reveals her path to self-discovery and personal power and shows us how to return to our personal garden and live on earth in a natural and balanced way. (Tradepaper $11.95)

Embracing Our Selves: The Voice Dialogue Manual. By Drs. Hal and Sidra Stone. The highly acclaimed, groundbreaking work that explains the psychology of the selves and the Voice Dialogue method. (Tradepaper $12.95)

Embracing Each Other: Relationship as Teacher, Healer and Guide. By Drs. Hal and Sidra Stone. A compassionate guide to understanding and improving our relationships. The follow-up to the Stone's pioneering book on Voice Dialogue. (Tradepaper $11.95)

The Shadow King: The Invisible Force that Holds Women Back. By Dr. Sidra Stone. This book teaches women how to transform the voice that echoes the values of patriarchy in our society so they can claim their full feminine power. (Tradepaper $12.95)

Maps to Ecstasy (Revised): A Healing Journey for the Untamed Spirit. By Gabrielle Roth, with John Loudon. A modern mystic shows us how to reconnect to the vital energetic core of our being through dance, song, theater, writing, meditation, and ritual. (Tradepaper $12.95)

Passion to Heal: The Ultimate Guide to Your Healing Journey. By Echo Bodine. An invaluable guide for mapping out our individual journeys to health. (Tradepaper $14.95)

Awakening the Warrior Within: Secrets of Personal Safety & Inner Security By Dawn Callan. This book explodes contemporary myths about attaining personal safety, revealing how they may actually contribute to our victimization, and introduces the Warrior Code—ten important keys for making the journey back to power. (Tradepaper $12.95)

Coming Home: The Return of True Self. By Martia Nelson. A down-to-earth spiritual primer that explains how we can use the cery flaws of our humanness to carry the vibrant energy of our true self and reach the potential that dwells in all of us. (Tradepaper $12.95)

Nataraj* Publishing, a division of New World Library
is dedicated to publishing books and cassettes
that inspire and challenge us to improve the quality
of our lives and our world.

For a catalog of our fine books and cassettes contact:

New World Library
14 Pamaron Way
Novato, CA 94949

Telephone: (415) 884-2100
Fax: (415) 884-2199
Or call toll-free (800) 972-6657
Catalog requests: Ext. 50
Ordering: Ext. 52

E-mail: escort@nwlib.com
http://www.nwlib.com

*Nataraj is a Sanskrit word referring to the creative, transformative power of the universe.